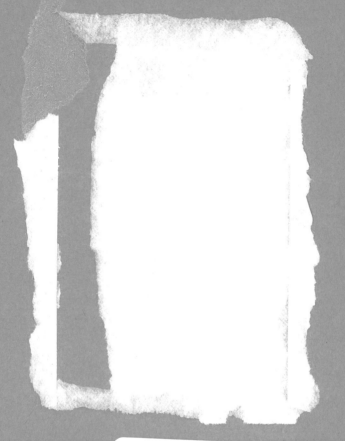

The European
Orders
of Chivalry

❖❖❖❖❖❖❖❖❖❖❖❖❖❖❖❖❖❖❖❖❖❖❖❖❖❖❖❖❖❖❖❖

❖❖❖❖❖❖❖❖❖❖❖❖❖❖❖❖❖❖❖❖❖❖❖❖❖❖❖❖❖❖

The European Orders of Chivalry

By
Gunnar Boalt, Robert Erikson,
Harry Glück, Herman Lantz

Southern Illinois University Press
Carbondale and Edwardsville

Printing subsidized by The Swedish Council for Social Science
Research (Statens Råd för Samhällsforskning)

Typography by Gudmund Nyström
Printed in Sweden
Kungl. Boktryckeriet P A Norstedt & Söner, Stockholm

Published in the United States of America
by the Southern Illinois University Press

International Standard Book Number 0-8093-0506-2
Library of Congress Catalogue Card Number 70-151002

Contents

Chapter 1
Sociology of Chivalrous Orders
Herman R. Lantz

Chivalrous orders, largely the concern of historians and genealogists, are of sociological relevance and significance for several reasons. First, at the most general level the manifestations of chivalrous orders are social products which provide knowledge about different historical periods. Chivalrous orders inform us about what people in the past considered important, the basis of their conflicts as well as their achievements.

A second reason why chivalrous orders are sociologically relevant is that they exemplify the most fundamental problems of social structure and social organization. From a sociological perspective these early orders, as their name suggests, represented a concern for the problems of *regulation, control and order*. The Hospitallers and the Templars, for example, each an early order, reacted to the excesses of the days of feudal society. This period, characterized by social instability and social chaos, was noted for the indifference of the lords to the weak and the poor. These chivalrous orders searched for balance and order in society through control. They emphasized Christian and spiritual concerns, rejecting worldly and material interests, and they tried to accomplish this by defending and rewarding those who accepted such values, and fighting those who were antagonistic to these views. In the course of these efforts to establish and maintain social order, a series of related problems arose, and each of these problems is also sociologically important.

Thus, a third reason why chivalrous orders are sociologically relevant is that they provide us with knowledge about the parameters of deviance. Such control of deviance was manifest in several ways. As already noted, the emergence of the order itself was generally in response to a moral cause, the preservation of a particular religion, or the protection of the poor and the sick. In addition, the behavior of individual members of the order was calculated to fulfill particular moral ideals. Undoubtedly deviations occurred, as will be noted later in this manuscript, but such deviations were often harshly dealt with, either by the princes who had sponsored the order, or by members of the order themselves. Especially relevant from a sociological perspective is the range of deviation in behavior which orders permitted before action was taken, a problem which this manuscript tries to undertake. Since deviation invariably foreshadowed social change, the change perspective becomes relevant.

Thus, a fourth reason sociologists are interested in chivalrous orders is that it affords them an opportunity to observe both the change and evolution of social structures. Such analysis is especially important because it is possible to understand better the dynamic nature of a social structure in response to social forces in a society be they economic, political, or religious. The change and evolution of chivalrous orders is noted in several ways. They exemplify the fact that organizational goals are not merely the products of those persons responsible for the order. Instead, goals are equally the by-products of ongoing social forces. Chivalrous orders, starting out with altruistic concerns, soon found themselves surrounded by the forces of social reality which altered and shaped their direction in ways difficult to predict at the time. The fact that orders could have persisted as they did with total concerns for the defense of Christianity and the protection of the poor suggests their firm belief that the "kingdom of heaven" was soon to become a reality. It is ironic that, as they pursued these goals, they became increasingly enmeshed in the very problems of morality which the orders were designed to avoid.

For example, in order to achieve even their basic goals, that is the defense of Christian pilgrims and Christianity itself, it was necessary to recruit large armies which ushered in a stage of militarism. Militarism was essentially functional for several reasons. Christian ethics were not sufficient to sustain people who had come from a set of worldly traditions. Perhaps for an initial period of time there may have been some satisfaction. Yet at least three things were lacking, the capacity to remain passive in a world which was hostile and torn with strife. To accept such a view undoubtedly would have contributed to restlessness and anxieties for the members of these orders. For whatever their Christian doctrine espoused, these people were not themselves saintly, and they saw around them the seeds and the actions of violent men. For them to remain passive and Christlike could only have symbolized death and martyrdom, a state they were not yet prepared to accept. Nor were they prepared to accept a second basic requirement of these orders, namely equality before Christ. These men came out of an age in which status differences were significant, and one in which power and wealth were the determinants of one's place in the social order. For most of these people the transition to a non-worldly, spiritual order was difficult, if not impossible.

Finally, few of these people were in fact prepared for the ascetic life, the life of abstinence and chastity. It may well be that militarism provided a rationalization for such worldly involvements not readily available. Thus, in some basic ways the original set of goals of chivalrous orders, and their structures as well, were soon to undergo drastic change.

Militarism and the bureaucracy surrounding military organization began to flourish. Military statuses and differentiation began to take place. While these developments fulfilled needs, as just outlined, they created internal conflict with the basic goals of Christian ethics which represented the foundation upon which the order itself was built. Such conflict and ambivalence continued for extensive periods of time and dissension within orders was present.

It is not surprising therefore to observe certain characteristic developments. Militarism became a successful endeavor organized along commercial lines in which orders became wealthy and powerful, establishing status differences between various orders and status differences within the orders themselves. The wealth of orders increased to such an extent that orders undertook certain basic banking functions, including the protection of, and the loaning of, money, presumably without direct charges of interest. Such growth in wealth was accompanied by political power involving the acquisition of ever larger amounts of territory through conquest and consolidation. Eventually, some orders grew to represent threats to political kingdoms, they became a state within a state. It became necessary for established monarchs to deal with orders either by reducing their power or by working out an accommodation through pledges of loyalty.

A fifth reason chivalrous orders have become sociologically relevant has to do with the social use which has been made of orders. Within a span of several centuries chivalrous orders passed through a number of changes in which goals originally oriented to the preservation of Christian ethics gave way to other concerns. Such changes encompassed a set of worldly goals for wealth, power and status. Had they pursued their original Christian goals, chivalrous orders would probably have found themselves destroyed or absorbed by religious orders. The pursuit of more aggressive, militaristic and commercial goals also meant that their power would become curbed by monarchs.

As nations became unified, orders were employed in several ways. First, while armies are not employed, the order as symbolized by the cross or medallion may still be awarded in order to achieve political unity. Some of these may go to persons for bravery in battle, others for civilian service. Yet each of these represents a chain of recommendations from those in power, who expect in return both support and political loyalty. As such the distribution of the number of orders in a given period, including even the creation of new orders, can be viewed as a sensitive barometer of conditions in a society. One finds, for example, that the flow of orders may be viewed in terms of a social change perspective. An increase in the number of orders appears to be correlated with a condition of political fluidity in which those in power are in need of support. In a similar vein, the physical composition, gold, silver, platinum, gems which are on the medallion, is also suggestive of both the status and intent. The more ornate and costly the medallion, the greater the significance of the award. One may therefore learn much about the social changes and stresses of a society by examining the flow and distribution of orders.

In general non-democratic societies who remain in power largely through support of particular political and military organizations have a greater distribution of orders than do democratic societies. Moreover, generally speaking, traditional societies with a history of orders have continued to employ them. In some respects, however, the function of an order in both the democratic and non-democratic society are not totally different. For example, every political regime, democratic or not, has a patronage system which awards very high ranking positions to people for political support. Among other things these often include ambassadorships to foreign countries, and it is well known that many of these positions are given to politically influential and helpful people for their part in political campaigns. In fact, this is so often the case that career service officers are very upset when they are by-passed by less talented, less knowledgeable, political figures who receive such appointments.

The Future

The future of orders will depend to a great extent on the direction which societies take, directions which are not easy to predict. First, it may well be that new societies undergoing political instability with needs for support may create new orders and reissue some old ones from possibly a colonial period which are still reputable.

Within the past two decades significant concerns for national autonomy and social identity have become manifest in an increase in the number of new political states around the world. Underlying reasons for such a development are related to the reappraisal of the goals and aims which larger nations have undertaken, and the consequent encouragement of ongoing nationalistic movements. If we can assume inevitable instability fostered by such movements, we can also assume that societies will make efforts to consolidate gains to control deviant political behavior. Thus, such efforts at control may take the form of issuing some type of order which will carry with it social status.

Thus, it may be that with the creation of new states, we shall have an increase in orders and such an increase may take place at an increasingly rapid rate. Older, but still youthful societies, may make use of orders under certain conditions. Any society which yearns for tradition and stability is a society that may come to look with favor upon orders. Such things might even come to pass in American society with a minimum of tradition. It would be interesting to know how much time is spent by professional genealogists and how much money is spent by Americans who wish to trace their ancestry. Many of the state historical libraries are deluged with visitors hoping to link their family lines to significant members in history. Moreover, men's clothing, ties and jackets with crests have become increasingly popular within the last decade.

In general, social conditions which may influence such phenomena as the distribution of orders have to be seen in a context of more basic moves toward or away from tradition.

In an older traditional society many people can find prestige and an identity by rejecting tradition, by minimizing the importance of orders. In such a society, there may be moves to reduce orders. In younger permissive societies caught in chaos and instability, there may be a yearning for tradition which represent stability. For example, it is ironic that the newer youth movements in America and elsewhere, that represent rejection of the older generation, involve a manner of dress much more characteristic of an earlier, presumably more stable age. Once a society moves in the direction of concern for tradition, one of the social ingredients compatible with a concern for orders is present. We observe here one of the most persistent problems of social organizations, the balance between the need for change and deviance and the need for order.

In this first section we have presented a sociological perspective on chivalrous orders. In this connection we have indicated that basic social process and problems that can be observed in society can be observed in the early formation of orders, and the symbolic use which has been or could be made of orders. In this regard one must look on chivalrous orders as one means of achieving social control. The use of orders may become purely symbolic, they may go in or out of fashion. Until such time as they disappear completely, they provide us with significant sociological data about human societies. In the sections which follow these sociological dimensions will be presented in detail.

Chapter 2
The Religious Orders
of Knighthood

Medieval history is fascinating but complicated. Only specialists, well versed in the original sources, familiar with the conflicting views on the events and trained in the technique to weed out unlikely interpretations, can be trusted to handle the data, select them and present them to critical readers. The sociologist, who moves into these fields, can make little use of his own techniques; the end result may reflect distortion and error. Nevertheless it need not end up quite that way. Sociology becomes relevant in at least two basic ways. A first has to do with the perspective concerned with the interrelationship of social forces and institutions into patterns of social change. Sociology my also be relevant in terms of method, the ordering and classifying of events which lend themselves to patterns. Our story starts with the first crusade.

The crusaders took the city of Jerusalem by storm on 15 July 1099. The Muslim defenders had expelled the Christians living in the city a week earlier, but probably at least one Christian was left in the city: Gerard, administrator of the hospital of St. John. The hospital was a part of a monastery, St. Mary of the Latins, but now was made a center for those engaged in hospital work. They formed an organization of their own, soon gained independance and in 1113 the Pope gave this new order a foundation charter. Gerard, the first Grand Master of the Order, died in 1120 and his successor, Raymond du Puy was—as the charter stated—chosen only by the professed brethren of St. John. Du Puy died some time between 1158—1160.

Riley-Smith (*The Knights of St. John in Jerusalem and Cyprus 1050—1310,* St. Martin's Press. New York 1947, p. 39—40) points out that the king as well as the Patriarch of Jerusalem repeatedly gave considerable resources to the order of the Hospitallers, as they now are called. "Reasons for this favor are not hard to find. With the Holy Sepulchre in Christian hands and pilgrimages now unimpeded, an organization dedicated to the care of pilgrims clearly had an admirable and useful purpose. The hospital in Jerusalem was already well known to pilgrims in the early twelfth century, and its fame quickly spread into Western Europe".

Fame gav more resources. By 1113 the order had large properties in Italy, Spain and Southern France; hospices opened at all the important Mediterranean ports where pilgrims and crusaders embarked for the Holy Land: Marseilles, Asti, Pisa, Bari, Otranto, Taranto and Messina. The Hospitallers formed the first of the international religious chivalry orders.

They also were the first to stress the goal of caring for the sick and the poor—and the second order to engage regularly in military activities. The reasons for that probably are many, but certainly the new order of the Templars set an example to the Hospitallers. The Templars are said to have started as a group of Frankish Knights, "who, being distressed by the sufferings of Christian pilgrims decided to devote their lives to the protection and aid of these people, as they made their way from Asia Minor and the sea ports of the eastern Mediterranean to the Holy City." (Thomas Parker: *The Knights Templars in England*. The University of Arizona Press, Tucson, 1963 p. 2). These knights took vows of poverty, chastity and obedience, but soon considered as their chief duty to fight against the infidels "whether or not Christian pilgrims were threatened". Baldwin II, king of Jerusalem gave them a residence near the church, called the Temple of Solomon, and thus they later were known as Knights of Christ and the Temple of Solomon of Jerusalem. They appealed to Bernhard of Clairvaux for aid, were recognized as an order in 1128 at Troyes; the church council leaving the revision of their constitution to Bernhard.

"Because of their fame arising from their soldierly skill which brought victory in battle and their religious enthusiasm which set an example of self sacrifice, and in addition, because of Bernhard's words of praise which were as unstinting as they were influential, the Templars soon found themselves besieged by recruits and patronized by kings, popes, princes, and other lords, both lay and ecclesiastical." Parker: *The Knights Templars in England*, 1963 p. 3.

The Templars grew in numbers and took over many important castles and strongholds in the Holy Land to garrison and administer according to the usual feudal system introduced by the crusaders. They were divided into several classes: Knights, recruited from noblemen, sergeants or lay brothers recruited from free men, chaplains or priests, craftsmen formed a fourth class and temporary members, taking the vows only for a limited time, can be said to form a fifth. Only the knights were allowed to wear the white mantle with the red cross, only they could be promoted to the office of preceptor, in command of a castle or manor and its surroundings. The preceptories of a country used to form a province, administered by a Grand prior with a provincial council at his side. The Grand Master in Jerusalem had the Seneschal as second in command, the Marshal responsible for military administration, the Commander of the realm of Jerusalem, at the same time treasurer of the order. At the side of the Grand Master and his chief officials stood the Council of the Order, where the Grand Master only had one vote but that might be enough, since he alone decided who should be members of his council. The order thus was organized hierarchically, each member blindly obeying the commands of his superiors and obeyed by his subordinates. The knights were a small part of the total force, serving as officers or as heavy cavalry, their squires recruited from the younger sergeants and the rest of the sergeants handling the less important offices in the administration or serving as foot soldiers.

This organization of the Templars was the same in all their provinces, but it originated in the Holy Land and might have been an adjustment to the situation there. The crusaders had taken Jerusalem and the important harbors in Palestine. The way was in one sense open to the pilgrims. The princes, lords and knights taking part in the crusade had gone to Jerusalem, had fulfilled their vows and then went back home to their feudal obligations and rights there. Weapons, clothes for the Mediterranean climate, fare and food had cost them enormous sums. They were eager to get the situation at home straightened out and their affairs in shape again—and to make use of the reputation they had won for themselves and their followers in the Holy Land.

Some of them of course were willing to stay in the new kingdom of Jerusalem; younger sons of the noble families often had no land of their own and of course some had joined the crusade in order to escape from obligations or even crimes. These crusaders were anxious for a new career, they might get attached to the royal court in Jerusalem or they might join the Templars, but they were only a small part of the army that had conquered Palestine. The main body of that army rapidly left. How was the king then to defend this new country of his? The usual feudal system gave the liege lord right to call in his vassals with their fixed number of sub vassals and/or followers to be used against an invader or an unloyal vassal. This worked well as long as the enemy used the same system, that is, mercenaries were few and comparatively expensive. The invader then had just as much time to use his vassals for a conquest as the defender to use his for the defense.

The situation was, however, different in Palestine. The kingdom of Jerusalem and its dependent countries, Tripoli etc., were surrounded by infidels, certainly also organized in a kind of feudal system, but in principle hostile and always to be watched. Cities and castles needed strong garrisons. Recruiting and handling expeditionary forces had to be planned in advance and it was seldom possible to release them when the theoretical time, 40 days had expired. This situation required a standing army; hence the Templars, the Hospitallers, the knights of Lazarus and the Teutonic knights all changed in that direction. They were not mercenaries to be paid in cash or liable to change sides in a feud. They were devoted Christians, bound to fight the infidels, to remain poor and unmarried, not to be shaken in their loyalty by domestic considerations. They were splendid soldiers and their obedience vow made them the only well disciplined troops in all Christianity. But they had to get their recruits and their resources from all Europe to spend them in the defense of the Holy Land, where the Muslims found it very difficult to resist the attacks of mailclad knights, able to stand ten times more of blows and arrows than any cavalry they had met before.

Riley-Smith points out, that the Hospitallers began their military activities as an extension of their charitable duties. These duties included protection of the pilgrim routes, at least the Hospitallers themselves seem to have thought so. The king as well as the lords of the Holy Land were anxious, however, to use the order's military strength and bought them with land and privileges, handling over the castles at the border, most difficult to defend. The warrior class within the order thus grew and probably "developed its own momentum". (Jonathan Riley-Smith: *The Knights of St. John in Jerusalem and Cyprus 1050—1310.* 1967, p. 55.)

This warrior class among the Hospitallers can be traced to the time of Raymond du Puy, the second Grand Master. Riley-Smith does not believe in an "early differentiation of the brothers into those who fought and those who did not. The only division known until 1206 was that into clerical and lay brethren. Indeed the early military duties may have been performed not by the brothers at all, but by paid mercenaries." In 1148, however, Gillebertus called himself knight and brother of the Hospitallers and in "1152 the Pope knew that there was a fighting element within the Hospital." Raymond du Puy probably introduced the military wing but intended it only for limited use. Pope Alexander III, between 1178 and 1180, ordered the Hospitallers not to bear arms "according to the custom of the said Raymond, except when the standard portraying the Holy Cross is carried for the defense of the Kingdom or for the siege of some pagan city."

The expansion of the military wing can be seen in the defensive tasks the Hospitallers took on. They accepted more and more castles at the border, castles with land and tenants, but castles to defend with large garrisons and costly equipment. The Grand master Gilbert d'Assailly advocated this policy. At the important council-of-war of the Jerusalem kingdom in 1168, he was able to influence the conduct of foreign policy as the council followed his advice to invade Egypt. The attack was beaten off and the order lost considerably in men and money. A party among the Hospitallers evidently were against the military policy and succeeded in persuading the chapter of the order to demand from the Grand Master a promise not to acquire new fortresses without its knowledge. The military policy did not change, however.

There were several classes of members in the order: brother priests, by the late twelfth century there were sisters of St. John, by the thirteenth century there were brother knights and sergeants. There were lay associates: confratres and donats. The brethren all lived in common houses, called convents, each led by a commander. The commanderies formed provinces, called priories, capitular commanderies or capitular castellaries, according to the title of the officer in charge. The Grand Master had eight Grand officers: the Grand Commander, the Marshal, the Treasurer, etc. and the Grand council with its counterparts at the provincial level. The knights' position steadily rose within the order: about 1237 brother knights got precedence over the priests, in 1262 the office of Grand master was reserved for knights and in the 1270's all high offices. The military wing thus took command, but at the same time was differentiated in the knights of noble descent and the sergeants.

Technically their organization in Europe is important, because their provinces were substituted by "tongues", that is, areas talking the same language, important for giving and understanding commands and selecting commanders. The military point of view thus came to dominate even this field.

The knights of the Templars wore a white mantle with a red cross; all Hospitallers wore a black mantle with an eight-pointed white cross. The third international military order, of St. Lazarus, was distinguished by a green cross and took care of the lepers, but they followed the same trend toward militarism as the Hospitallers, remaining a small order, though. The Hospitallers treated illness of their own members in their hospitals, but not the lepers. They were handed over to the order of St. Lazarus.

There also was an order of English knights, dedicated to St. Thomas the Martyr. These knights followed the rules of the Templars and wore a red and white cross on their mantles. (Stubbs: *Lectures in Medieval History*, pp. 182—5.)

The Teutonic Order (Deutscher Ritterorden) started with a fraternity of German laymen who nursed their sick compatriots when the crusaders besieged Acre in 1191. After the conquest of Acre they acquired a hospital there and were approved by the Pope as an order of their own. The militarization of this order came in 1198. The knights wore white mantles with a black cross.

The transformation of these orders into fighting, recruiting and resource collecting machines took a long time. Once established, the new kingdom of Jerusalem remained for a time relatively secure, since its neighbors, Damascus and Egypt, were weak and unable to cooperate against the Christians. The situation changed, however. Let us have a look at the history of the crusaders, trying to focus on the role of the military orders . . .

The Crusaders and the Military Orders

Godfrey of Bouillon, the first ruler of Jerusalem, died in 1100. His brother, Baldwin I succeeded him, expanded the kingdom and died in 1118. Baldwin II integrated the conquests. The kings were elected by the royal council, which, however, showed great respect for the royal line, even when they had to accept a son in law, instead of a son. There was a Latin church, headed by the patriarch of Jerusalem. The military orders, represented by their Grand masters, got considerable influence in the royal council. The harbors held large

The Religious Orders of Knighthood

colonies of Italian merchants, living on shipping and commerce. North of the kingdom lay the county of Tripoli, small but important for its trade, the principality of Antiochia and the county of Edessa, all Christian and etablished during the first crusade. These four states never had more than 2000—3000 noblemen and priests to govern them, the majority coming from France. The Muslims formed a large part of the population especially in the Northern states.

The leading Muslim states in the Near East were the Abbasidian caliphate of Bagdad and the Fatimide caliphate of Cairo. None of them cared very much about the Christians. The smaller Turkish states of Aleppo and Damascus did care, but they were weak and often at war with one another.

The ambitious governor of Mosul, Zengi, brought, however, Aleppo back to Bagdad's control and then conquered the county of Edessa in 1114. This set off the second crusade, a crusade started by Louis VII of France who made the pope Eugenius III, Bernhard of Clairvaux and the German king, Conrad III, to accept his plans. (Paul Lesourd and Jean Marie Ramiz: *On the Path of the Crusaders*. Massada. Israel 1969, pp. 59—83.)

Conrad started in spring 1147 to march through Hungary, Balkan, Asia Minor and then was ambushed by the Turks. King Louis was beaten early in 1148. Both kings arrived, however, with small forces to the Holy Land, performed their devotions at the Holy Sepulchre and then attacked Damascus. The military orders sent large contingents to this army, and when it was defeated, the Templars could be given the blame. King Louis, however, wrote to Suger, bishop of St. Denis, that he could not have "existed even the shortest time" without them (Thomas Parker: *The Knights Templars in England*. The University of Arizona Press. Tucson. 1963 p. 10).

The second crusade was no success, but it brought men and resources to the orders, especially to the Templars, who took hold of the city fortresses of Ascalon and Gaza in 1149. Zengi's son, Nureddin, succeeded to unite Damascus with the rest of Syria against the "Franks" in 1154. Fatimid Egypt, however, still had not taken sides in the controversy and both parties tried to gain control over it. King Amalric I of Jerusalem attacked the Nile delta several times between 1163 and 1168. Nureddin sent his general Shirquh each time to help Cairo repel the invaders. In 1169 Shirquh entered Cairo and was made vizier to the Fatimid caliph. He died in the same year, but was succeeded by his nephew, Saladin, who in 1171 deposed of the last Fatimid caliph and proclaimed the Abbasid caliphate in Egypt.

Nureddin died in 1174 and Saladin quickly seized Damascus, in 1183 he took control of Aleppo and in 1186 of Mosul. He then had resources for his religious goal: the expulsion of the Christians. He launched his attack in 1187, decisively beat the Christian forces at Hattin, and then conquered one castle after another. Jerusalem fell in October 1187. In two years Saladin had taken all four of the Christian states. Only Tyre, Tripoli and some castles still remained in Christian hands; hence the third crusade.

The first counterattack came in 1189, when the Franks took back considerable parts of the coast and started the siege of Acre. Pope Gregory VIII called for a new crusade. Richard Coeur de Lion, Philip Augustus of France and the emperor Frederick Barbarossa all accepted the cross and went to the Holy Land; the two kings by ship, the emperor through Hungary and Byzans. Frederick drowned in the river Saleph and only a small part of his forces reached the Holy Land to take part in the siege of Acre.

Philip Augustus arrived to Acre in 1191. Richard Coeur de Lion landed in Cyprus and conquered the island from its self-styled emperor, Isaac Comnenus. He then took his forces down to Acre, that fell a month later. Philip Augustus went home, but Richard stayed on, recovering more harbors, but not able to attack Jerusalem. When Guy de Lusignan was deposed of as king of Jerusalem in 1192, Richard helped him to establish a kingdom of Cyprus (taken over by Venice in 1489).

Saladin died in 1193 and his empire fell to parts again, thus making the surival of the Latin settlement for another century possible. By this time the king and the nobles had small resources. Only the military orders could still mobilize recruits and ship money from their European bases. Their influence and power grew rapidly.

The remnants of Barbarossa's army returned home after the conquest of Acre, but some of the Germans remained and organized their hospital there as a military order, The Teutonic Knights, in 1198. The order received privileges, land and castles, among them, north of Acre, Montfort, where the High Master of the order took his seat. In 1210 Herman von Salza was elected High Master. He realized that the orders were not strong enough to take Jerusalem back and too far from their bases in Europe. He therefore accepted the offer from Hungary to conquer and convert the Kumans at the

The Religious Orders of Knighthood

Transylvanian border. This did not turn out well, since the order was expelled from Hungary in 1225, but a better offer came from duke Conrad of Mazovia: to organize a crusade against the Prussians. And so the order took little part of the fighting in the Holy Land after 1225, although the High Master resided in Montfort until it fell in 1271.

The third crusade accomplished little, and a new crusade, the fourth, was preached. It started in 1199, but in a wrong direction: the Venetians transported the eager knights first to Hungarian Zara; stormed and sacked in 1202, then to Constantinople, stormed and sacked in 1204. The pope had to call for a fifth crusade. Emperor Frederick II took the cross in 1215, but did not join the forces that sailed out in 1218 against Egypt to take the important harbor of Damietta and try to exchange it for Jerusalem. Damietta was taken, but the crusaders had to leave it in 1221 and return to Acre. Hospitallers and Templars took part of the operations and in the councils of war, but their role at Damietta is not quite clear.

Emperor Frederick II did not start for the Holy Land until in 1227. His fleet arrived to Acre, but he himself had turned back, which made the pope excommunicate him. His wife, Yolande, was heiress of the Jerusalem kingdom, but neither the barons there, nor the Templars or the Hospitallers appreciated his autocratic leadership. Only the Teutonic knights remained loyal to their emperor. When he marched for Jerusalem, Templars and Hospitallers marched too, but at a distance from the excommunicated emperor. This did not make sense from the military point of view, not even to the orders themselves, and they joined forces with the emperor on condition that all commands should be issued not in his name, but in the name of God and Christendom.

The emperor's name and diplomatic skill, more than his army, won Jerusalem, Nasareth, Bethlehem and a corridor to Jaffna back to the kingdom with a peace for 10 years. The treaty, ending the sixth crusade, was signed without Templars' or Hospitallers' ratification, which turned them against Frederick. The Pope started a new somewhat peculiar crusade in Italy: against Frederick's possessions, and the Italian provinces of Templars as well as Hospitallers joined this crusade. Frederick then returned to Italy and his first act was to seize all possessions of Templars in Apulia. The Templars in the Holy Land revenged this by expelling the Teutonic knights from Acre.

Turkish troops in Egyptian pay took back Jerusalem in 1244. The same year king Louis IX of France took the cross and in 1248 he sailed for Egypt, hoping to catch Damietta and exchange it for Jerusalem.

This seventh crusade thus repeated the fifth and ended just as badly. Louis took Damietta in 1249. In 1250 he himself was captured and had to ransom himself and his fellow prisoners with Damietta and all money available in the ships, most of it belonging to the Templars, who lost not only their treasure, but also their Grand Master and many knights in the bitter fighting. Louis then went to Palestine but achieved little and returned to France in 1254. The long rivalry between Templars and Hospitallers then broke out into open warfare. The three large military orders often came in conflict with one another, but actual fighting was against their common cause. They saw this at last and in 1258 they made a treaty laying down rules how to settle disputes, help one another in war, etc. The pope confirmed the treaty in 1275 and it evidently worked in practice the short period left to the orders in Palestine.

By this time the sultans of Egypt had organized slave troops, Mamelucks, and when the mongols captured and sacked Bagdad, killing the last Abbasid caliph, in 1258, the Mamelucks, commanded by Baybars, met the mongols in 1260 at Ayn Jalut and defeated them. The Christians had sided with the mongols, so Baybars attacked them, storming one stronghold after another. The eighth crusade under the leadership of Louis IX made him hesitate, but Louis went in 1270 to Tunisia, out of harm's way, where he died. The Mamelucks resumed their offensive. In 1291 they attacked Acre, defended by Templars, Hospitallers, Teutonic knights and knights of St. Thomas of Acre to the bitter end, when the city was taken by storm, sacked and razed to the ground. The Grand Master of the Hospitallers was wounded and carried off to Cyprus in a ship. The Grand Master of the Templars was killed and their Marshal sent the treasure of the order to Cyprus. There Templars and Hospitallers set up their new headquarters.

The Hospitallers took part in some small expeditions against the Muslims, but started to reduce their own number. In 1292 new knights were allowed to enter the order only by a permission from the Grand Master or the Grand Commander. The order probably tried to adjust to naval warfare, made natural by its seat on an island. Their fleet grew rapidly. In 1299 the first Admiral of the

Hospital was appointed. In 1306 a small Hospitaller fleet attacked Rhodes and some years later the whole island and the city was in their hands. The order moved their headquarters to Rhodes in 1309.

The Templars fared worse. Philip the Fair, King of France, accused them in 1305 of sinful living. Their Grand Master, James de Molay, was called to France to discuss plans for a new crusade, and there he still was when the pope announced that at the request of the Grand Master, he had decided to investigate the accusations against the order. This was made public on the 24 August, 1307. On 13 October all the Templars in France were arrested, also their Grand Master. The French inquisition war brought in, used torture and some of the knights confessed enormous sins. The pope did not take these confessions very seriously, but the French inquisitors did and used them to burn the Grand Master and the Commander of Normandy. The pope then dissolved the order, although they had not been formally found guilty.

The property of the Templars in all countries but Spain and Portugal was to be turned over to the Hospitallers. They won what the Templars lost. But they now knew their peril and were careful not to overdo their collecting, passing by what the French king or his important courtiers had taken over, and using a similar policy in England (see Parker: *The Knights Templars in England*, pp. 103, 104.)

The Military Orders after the Crusades

The pope did not transfer the Templar possessions in Castile, Aragon or Portugal to the Hospitallers. Why not? Because these countries were fighting the infidels in Southern Spain since a long time. They already had a number of military orders, formed for this purpose and recognized by the pope.

The order of Calatrava had been instituted in 1158, the order of Aviz in 1160, the order of St. James in 1170 and the order of Alcantara in 1176. The order of St. James was founded to protect pilgrims going to the relique shrine of the apostle St. James at Compostella. The three other orders had their names from the fortified cities they were holding against the moors. All of them were, however, founded long after the Templars and the Hospitallers. These two senior orders both had lands and castles in the Peninsula. When Alphonse I of Aragon died in 1134, he made them heirs of his kingdom. This did not quite come off, as he was succeeded by Ramiro II. The kings of Castile were not up to the generosity of Aragon, but when Alphonse VII stormed Calatrava (Ciudad Real), he gave it to the Templars to defend, on the usual conditions. The Templars gratefully accepted, but some years later, they found that this important fortress cost them more than they cared for. They told the king, Sancho II, that their resources were not large enough to hold Calatrava. Raimundo de Fitero and Diego Velasquez asked the king's permission to take over the fortress and started a crusade to save Calatrava, out of which the order of Calatrava arose, in several ways following the pattern of the Templars. Alphonse VIII is said to have organized the knights of Calatrava as well as the knights of St. James (Santiago).

The property of the Templars in Castile probably was taken over by the three orders with headquarters there. In Aragon, however, the order of Montesat was created in 1316 and it seems likely that this order was formed just to keep the Aragon Templar property togeth-er—and to prevent the orders of Calatrava, St. James and Alcantara, all of them seated in Castile, to take over. The order of Montesat in this sense is the successor of the Templars. It is even possible that members of the Templars passed into the order of Montesat.

Portugal acted the same way as Aragon. The orders of Calatrava, St. James and Alcantara had large possessions there and so had of course the order of Aviz, with its headquarter in Portugal. The king of Portugal, Dionysios, never accepted the accusations against the Templars, and their property he gave to the new order of Christ, cre-ated in 1317. The Templars' tradition might have passed into this order and the name, order of Christ, might be a shortened form of the order of Christ and the Temple of Solomon of Jerusalem. The pope confirmed the order some years later, on the condition that the Holy See also got the right to appoint knights of Christ.

Just as in the Holy Land the Military orders garrisoned the strong-holds against the Muslims in Spain, recruited knights and men for the expeditions and acquired land and money to build up their base organizations. Most of them had possessions in all the Christian Kingdoms of the Iberian Peninsula. This made them constant parts in the conflicts between and within the kingdoms. The marriage of Ferdinand and Isabella united Aragon and Castile to Spain. The last Moorish lands were conquered, and then there were no frontiers left for the orders. They had considerable resources and power, how-ever. Isabella persuaded the pope to give her the right to appoint

Grand Masters of Calatrava, St. James and Alcantara. She appointed king Ferdinand to all three when the former Grand Masters passed out. The order of Montesat was taken over by the Spanish crown somewhat later. The King of Spain thus built up a financial position in a similar way as the protestant kings later did when they took over the property of the catholic church in their countries. But Isabella's way did not offend the church and was strictly legal, and the orders had to accept it. The king of Portugal soon used the same technique and so got control of the land belonging to the Portuguese military orders.

The military orders evidently needed a frontier, held against infidels and heathens; they also needed to be backed up by Papal authority. The Byzantines had no military orders, but a standing army. When the Russians got a border to defend against the Turks, this task was taken over by the cossacks. The only heathen territories remaining for the expansion of the military orders in Europe were Prussia, Lithuania, Livonia. We have already seen that the Grand Master of the Teutonic knights, Herman von Salza, seized this opportunity, when duke Conrad of Mazovia presented it to him. The pope had previously declared, that the heathen Baltic peoples of course should be converted but not deprived of their freedom. They should remain peasants, not serfs. This was an obstacle for the plans of von Salza, so he secured in 1226 a charter from the emperor, Frederick II, giving the Teutonic knights the land they conquered from the heathen tribes. The conquest then started, the knights providing organization and leadership but not fighting men, as the conquests were made by German crusaders, taking the cross for a restricted time.

The heathen Prussians fought well, and when they found out what treatment they could expect from the conquerors, they fought in despair. The invasion started in 1231, in 1233 a general crusade followed. Castles were built, towns with German population founded, the conquered Prussians were badly handled unless they acknowledged the new rulers. In 1261 the Prussians rebelled and fierce fighting took place for 20 years, until the knights reestablished their control.

The bishop of Riga had in 1202 founded the military order of the Knights of the Sword, which controlled southern Esthonia and Livonia. This order was united with the Teutonic knights in 1237 but Livonia and Prussia were connected only by a narrow strip of coast, as Lithuania was strong enough to keep off the knights.

Poland was not too friendly either. The knights tried to expand into Russia but were beaten by Alexander Newski on Peipus in 1242.

Prince Jagiello of Lithuania married the Polish queen Jadwiga, united the two countries and accepted Christendom. The knights then had no excuse for a crusade and they were not able to withstand the pressure of the new Polish kings. They succeeded to get support and knights from many European countries but were decisively beaten in 1410 at Grunwald (Tannenberg) where the High Master was killed.

The headquarters of the order had moved to Venice, when Acre fell in 1291. The fate of the Templar might have influenced the High Master to move to Marienburg in Prussia at the delta of Vistula. The possessions of the order in Prussia were administered by the High Master himself, those in Esthonia, Courland and Livonia by a Landmaster and the lands at Rhine by a German Master (Deutsch meister). The reformation made the situation of the Teutonic order extremely difficult. The last High Master, Albert von Hohenzollern, dissolved the order in Prussia and made it a duchy for himself under Polish suzerainity. The Landmaster of Livonia tried to hold his province together, but in 1558 most of it was taken by Sweden, Russia or Poland. In 1561 the last Landmaster, Gotthard Kettler, gave up and became duke of Courland under Polish suzerainity. Only the German Master was left, as one of the ecclesiastic princes of the Holy Roman Empire, residing in Mergentheim. There the order survived until 1809.

There are no data about the English order of St. Thomas the Martyr of Acre after the conquest of that fortress; the order of Lazarus, however, moved their headquarters to Naples in 1311.

And now let us return to the Hospitallers once more. They had moved their headquarters to Limassol in Cyprus in 1291. At the chapter-general in Kolossi nearby, their future policy was decided: to take care of the sick and the pilgrims, to fight the infidels and to remain near the Holy Land so as to use the chance to reconquer it. The Grand Master Guillaume de Villaret had a new set of statutes worked out and carried through, adapting the order to their new situation. The Hospitallers used their new fleet to attack Rhodes in 1306. The capital city of the island is also called Rhodes and in 1309 it was in the hands of the Hospitallers, who fortified their new headquarter. It was made an efficient base for naval war against the Turks.

When the Turks hade conquered Constantinople, Rhodes was placed on the important ship route between the new Turkish capital and the Levant. The Turks had to take it. Mohammed II attacked and laid siege to the fortress in 1480. He was repulsed with heavy losses. Suleiman I succeeded to take it in 1523, but is said to have lost 90,000 men out of his army of 200,000.

The Grand Master, Philip Villiers de l'Isle Adam, evacuated the remains of his fortress under an honorable capitulation and went with his ships first to Candia, then to Sicily and Italy. The Grand Master himself visited several important European courts, was received with great honor but got little help. The emperor Charles V, however, seems to have been anxious to reduce his own military commitments against the infidels. He offered Malta and Tripoli in Africa (not the Tripoli north of Jerusalem). Villiers de l'Isle Adam was not enthusiastic. Tripoli, with a poor harbor and bad fortifications, was dangerous to accept. Malta, whith two fine harbors, might do if it was heavily fortified. The Grand Master accepted the imperial offer: Malta, Gozo, Comino and Tripoli, "to be held in fief noble, free and franc from military service". The emperor was to receive a falcon once a year, but the Hospitallers carefully guarded their sovereignity. They provided the falcon, but "only as a kind of perpetual memorial for benefits received". (Elizabeth W. Schmerhorn: *Malta of the Knights.* Heinemann, London, 1929, p. 35.)

The Hospitallers were divided into 8 "tongues" (langues) according to the language for commands; Aragon, Castile, Italy, Germany, England, Auvergne, Provence and France. These tongues were often opposed to one another and the dispute about the offer of the emperor nearly broke up the order. The French and the German tongues feared that the gift of Charles V would give to much influence to the Spanish tongues, which threatened to secede if the gift was rejected. The Grand Master pointed out that if the order were to remain a sovereign order, it must settle somewhere and in October, 1530 the old fleet from Rhodes sailed for Malta.

Villiers de l'Isle Adam had little treasure left after the wanderings of the order. Fortification works must go slow so he started with strengthening the fort of St. Angelo. The money problem was made worse, when Henry VIII in England took over the property of the order there. A number of English Hospitallers fled to Malta and had to be taken care of. Then Saxony, Brandenburg, Brunswick, Denmark and Sweden left the catholic church and confiscated the possession of the Hospitallers, which did not improve their situation.

Tripoli proved difficult to defend. A Turkish corsair, Dragut, conquered it in 1551. The Hospitallers' fleet based on Malta, however, soon was a serious threat to the Muslims' shipping along the north coast of Africa. Sultan Suliman equipped a large fleet to take Malta. The Grand Master Jean de la Valetta-Parisot got tidings of the preparations and started strengthening the fortifications, calling to Malta all his knights and resources. The Turkish fleet arrived in May 1565 with an army, 30,000 men strong. They succeeded in storming the little fort St. Elmo, but the main fortress, the Borgo, held out, defended by La Valetta himself, until relief from Sicily came in September and forced the Turks to give up the siege. It is said to have cost them 30,000 men, while the Christian losses were about 9000.

The Turks never repeated their attack, but the Hospitallers built on the place of St. Elmo a city and an enormous fortress, that was given the name La Valetta. The knights remained at Malta unmolested, as a relict from medieval time. During the eighteenth century Russians, Englishmen and Frenchmen used or misused the harbor of Valetta, caring little for the order.

The French revolution deprived the order of large revenues. Work stopped in the shipyard, the silver of the hospital had to be sold. In 1797 a new and weak Grand Master, Ferdinand von Hompesch, was elected. Bonaparte on board the Toulon fleet on his way to Egypt anchored in La Valetta in June 1798. A sortie, 900 men strong, was easily repulsed by Marmont. Then the knights gave up. Only the governor of Gozo defended his castle properly. And so the order lost Malta, never to recover it. The remaining possessions at the Rhine were lost to France and its allies in 1809.

The Sociological Points of View

Historians will find little that is new thus far. Orders are organizations, created for certain purposes and they belong to the times of feudalism in Catholic countries. Orders shared the religious goals of Catholic Europe and accepted the rules of Chivalry as they took form, especially in France. Military orders combined chivalric and religious goals to protect pilgrims and religious shrines. What we find therefore is that these orders just like most other organizations, evolve and undergo changes in goals. Etzioni *(Modern Organizations,* Prentice

The Religious Orders of Knighthood

Hall, Englewood Cliffs, 1964, pp. 10—14) uses the terms: displacement of goals, goal succession, multiplication and expansion and eventually multi-purpose organizations. We have already noted, how the Hospitallers added military performance to their hospitality and care, how militarism grew and soon dominated their organization. The Templars in the same way started with protection but soon were fighting infidels anywhere. The original goals were not displaced, they were still there and important but a new goal had been added to the original ones: fighting infidels. This military goal necessitated fighting men.

To recruit knights and sergeants was easy; the fame of Templars and Hospitallers brought them more recruits than they could accept and they probably preferred those of high ability or high nobility. The noble families could honorably get rid of younger sons, not anxious to join the Church, by giving them the chance to join the Templars or Hospitallers just as they later used the officer's career for them. But the recruits needed horses, weapons, ships and castles. Crusaders, pilgrims and would-be pilgrims were apt to need all the service the order could give them and so willing, nay anxious, to give land and property to the official representatives of the order. These commanders thus built up their local resources, using their privileges to escape taxes and road tolls, coming out as dangerous competitors to the merchants. Their international contact system made them just as dangerous to the bankers. Princes borrowed money from them and Philip the Fair had his treasure deposited in the Old Temple of Paris.

We use Thomas Parker: *The Knights Templars in England* (The University of Arizona Press, Tucson, 1963) to illustrate the financial operations at the New Temple in London. The Temple included a large storehouse, where valuables could be placed for safekeeping by the king or members of the nobility. King John deposited the royal jewels there (1204—1205), so did Henry III in 1232. Taxes were often transported to the Temple and stored there. Hubert de Burgh, justiciar to Henry III, left his fortune in the custody of the Templars, but the King deprived him his office, threw him in prison and then demanded his treasure to be handed over (1232). The Master of the Temple kept to his rules and said he could not do so without written instruction from the depositor with his signature or seal, date, name of payee and sum. Evidently the New Temple worked this way as a check account, but the king in this case needed the money so badly that he was prepared either to use torture to get de Burgh's signature or force to take the treasure. Hubert de Burgh, however, consented to the king's demand, and so the Templars did not need to give up their principles—this time.

The Templars also gave loans, often to the king, and probably they took the money from the deposited funds or out of their own revenues. Loans generally were to be paid back a certain day.

Did the Templars take interest? It was usury, a serious crime against the Canon Law, to do so. The Canon lawyers said and meant that no person should ask for more money to be returned than he had given the debtor. There were, however, two loopholes open. The creditor might accept a "free gift" from the debtor, if he had neither expected nor hoped for such a gift. The second opportunity came, if the debtor did not pay his loan back at the time agreed upon. Then the creditor could have an extra sum. Parker gives examples of both techniques and finds it "conceivable, though there seems to be no specific evidence, that the Templars were accustomed to receive such gifts for their grace in lending" (p. 71).

Money transports were difficult and dangerous in the Middle Ages. The Templars were trustworthy in this respect too, but if money was deposited at New Temple in London, another Templar house on the continent could discharge that sum to the designated party abroad. Templars also used credit letters. Parker points out, that while the Templars were not professional bankers, they were forced by their wealth and contacts into banking, thus they "are to be seen as financial leaders, especially in banking and credit activities, with few peers or significant rivals during much of the period" (p. 79).

To the goal of hospitality and the goal of protection the goal of economic power was added, with this political power emerged as well. Templars, Hospitallers and Teutonic knights played very important roles in the policy of the Jerusalem kingdom and in the states north of it too.

Hugh de Payens, the first Grand Master of the Templars, in 1128 visited King Henry I of England in Normandy, was generously received and went on to England and Scotland. The first grants to the order left in the registers, were made in 1137 and the enthusiasm of the crusades helped them greatly. "On the other hand, the Templars seem to have played shrewd politics during the period of civil turmoil, serving both parties and winning rewards from both sides, as charters and documents favoring the Templars, about sixty of which have survived, attest" (p. 16). Richard Coeur-de-Lion granted them considerable privileges, such as exemption from taxes on land and tallages, from payment of tolls on bridges and highways, import of wine without customs duties or export of wool to Flanders without duty, their own courts with full jurisdiction over their tenants and they could be impleaded only before the king or his chief justice. Some of these privileges remained on the paper and generally the Templars had to pay dearly for the recognition of their rights. A considerable part of their income in England had to be invested in Royal grace.

During the third crusade King Richard "found the Templars loyal allies, as was especially proved at Ascalon. When Richard returned to Europe in 1192, it was in a boat provided by Robert de Sable, Grand Master of the Templars. Wearing the habit of a Templar, and accompanied by four Templars and a number of attendants, he sailed first to Corfu and then to the northern shore of the Adriatic Sea, where he finally landed in the area Aquilcia and Venice. Retaining his Templar disguise and accompanied initially by several priests and two Templars, but later only by one attendant—in order to make capture less likely—the English monarch proceeded inland through territory belonging to his enemy, Leopold, Archduke of Austria." (Thomas Parker: *The Knights Templars in England.* 1 p. 47.)

Later King John, Richard's younger brother, often was a guest at the New Temple in London and relied on them for advice. New Temple seems to have been used often for important meetings. The parliament of 1272, met there, so did the parliament of 1299. The Master of the Temple in England regularly attended the Parliament sessions. "From 1295 to 1306 he was summoned by name, along with other leading clerics and lay lords, to be present;" (p. 48).

The Hospitallers and other great military orders had of course just as much political ambition as the Templars—or more. The military orders certainly had political influence and strength as a goal, succeeding the goal of military success and economic strength.

We have presented a number of points in order to demonstrate that the military orders can be assigned a number of goals operating within the sphere of the general religious and feudal value system in Europe. They started out to take care of and protect the pilgrims and the religious shrines. To do this efficiently they took on the goal to fight the infidels and this brought the goal of economic strength and then political strength. Status came with their fame. These goals easily combine, but not in all cases. We have to look at the possible goal conflicts.

Goal Conflicts in the Military Orders

Let us begin with the first goal of the orders: to take care of the pilgrims and the sick. This goal of hospitality was easily combined with the next goal: military strength. The Hospitallers, however, found it difficult to keep these two goals in balance, as the knights took over more and more important posts, until they had in practice a monopoly of all the high offices, the so called grand crosses, since these officers carried on their mantles a larger cross than knights and brethren of the order. The leadership of the knights could not be challenged, as long as they did not neglect the goal of hospitality—and as long as the military goal brought rewards to the order. But remember the action taken by the chapter of the order against the Grand Master d'Assailly after his disastrous expedition to Egypt in 1168, together with the forces of king Amalric of Jerusalem. The Grand Master was forced to promise not to take over new fortresses, that is, not to allocate more resources to the military goal. But in the future no reactions of this kind appear, until the order lost Malta in a way that gave little credit to the fighting spirit of the knights. Then the hospitality goal once more dominated. The knights organized military hospitals and ambulances, using their sovereignity and surviving status to mark their neutral property with their white Maltese crosses, that thus they needed no military protection and could serve both of the combattants. Still, the resources of the order were small and the expanding European armies met heavy casualties in battles. The Red Cross organization succeeded in building up an efficient hospital service, but it certainly took over many useful points from the Hospitallers. These illustrations can be said to demonstrate conflicts between the hospitality goal and the goal of military strength.

The military goal in these times needed such vast sums of money, that the economic goal is easy to recognize in the actions of the orders. It is, however, difficult to demonstrate a conflict between the goal of hospitality and the goal of economic strength. The Hospitallers seem to have taken their caring for the sick seriously and they gave away food and clothes on a scale that impressed their contemporaries. The Templars are sometimes accused of "greed for land", but not for greed in their care of pilgrims. The only case, that could be cited as at conflict between the hospitality goal and the goal of economic strength, is the little known scandal in the south of Italy concerning the order of St. Lazarus. The knights of St. Lazarus had to take care of the lepers, keeping them in isolated hospitals, "Lazarettes." The pope in about 1560 was disturbed by the persistent rumors, that the knights of the order used their power to seize and isolate lepers for the purpose of extortion. Victims, suffering from no other malady than too much money, had to pay them handsome sums to avoid the hospitality of the lazarettes. It is difficult to say, what proportions this misuse had. The pope considered it necessary to reform the order and when duke Charles Emanuel I of Savoy asked him to give official recognition to the revived order of St. Maurice, the pope did so only on the conditions that the Italian branch of the knights of St. Lazarus was included in the order and the Grand Mastership of the new order of St. Maurice and St. Lazarus vested in the crown of Savoy (1572).

We are unable to find good examples of conflicts between the hospitality goal and the political goal of the orders and so we turn to the goal of military strength and conflicting economic and/or politic goals. The Templars furnish us with a fine example. The military goal was to fight the infidels in the Holy Land, the goal of hospitality was to bring the pilgrims safe and sound to Jerusalem and back. Well handled this traffic gave a good profit. When the Muslims took Jerusalem back, the goals of the Templars came in conflict. The military goal could be realized only by reconquering Jerusalem and the Holy places. The Templars lacked the strength for that and if they kept trying, no pilgrims could get through and the traffic would stop. They took political contacts with some Muslim states, especially Damascus. They bribed the Muslim governors to let their special caravans through—and they certainly were accused as being traitors, accused by the emperor Frederick II, accused by the count of Artois before the battle of Mamourah in 1250: "See, the chance of capturing the sultan is open to us, and the ruin of all paganism is imminent, as well as the lasting exaltation of the Christian faith, all of which this Templar, who is present here, endeavors to impede by his fictitious and fallacious arguments. For the Templars and Hospitallers, and their associates, fear that: if the country is reduced to submission to the Christian power, their domination, who fatten on its rich revenues, will expire. Hence it is that they poison, in divers ways, the Christians who come hither girt for the cause of the cross, and, confederating with the Saracens, put them to death by various means. Is not Frederick who has had experience of their treachery, a most certain witness in this matter?" (Parker: *The Knights Templars in England*, the University of Arizona Press, Tucson, 1963, p. 109.) All these accusations had a core of truth: neither the Templars, nor the Hospitallers were anxious to be saddled with the responsibility for a large army of crusaders, lead by princes in conflict with one another, conquering cities and fortresses, difficult or impossible to defend the moment the crusaders, having gained their object, left the Holy Land again, as poor and defenseless, as it was when they arrived, but with a far larger burden of defense and Muslim neighbors more revengeful than before, especially if they had trusted the military orders earlier. The military goal of the orders thus could and repeatedly did come in conflict with their goals of hospitality, economic and political strength and stability.

The goal of economic strength in reality is a very complicated thing, just as complicated as political strength. An economic goal like buying additional land to establish a new commandery of course is in conflict with other economic goals such as acquiring new ships for the import of wine from Bordeaux to London. Allocation of resources simply means that different goals compete and that some of them are allotted more resources, others less. The same would hold for the interplay of political goals, which easily come in conflict with one another.

The easiest illustration probably is the way the military orders reestablished their headquarters, when they had been driven out of Acre in 1291. Temporarily they moved to Cyprus, where they all held some castles, but the kings of Cyprus were anxious not to let them buy land or expand their strength, as that would have given them too much influence in Cyprus affairs. The Hospitallers moved to Rhodes, which cost them enormous sums in fortifications and ships, but gave them political strength and independence. The Templars remained in Cyprus, planning a new crusade and building up their economic strength in Western Europe, especially in France. The catastrophy in 1305, when Pilip the Fair of France accused the order of sinful living, imprisoned all the Templars in his country and grasped their property, can be seen as a reaction in Europe against the solution the Templars had chosen to their goal conflict. They no longer protected pilgrims, fought infidels or had a foreign policy of their own. Instead they acquired land and money, building up their resources, which made them potentially powerful and dangerous within all Catholic countries and most dangerous to France, while at the same time they were vulnerable, a tempting prey and politically isolated, having no supporter but the Pope. Once Philip the Fair was able to overcome him, the Templars were lost.

The Hospitallers were driven out of Rhodes in 1523. They were offered several places for their headquarters, many of which were attractive from the economic point of view. These offers, however, the order did not accept, since they then had been forced to accept a king as their liege lord, to fight for him in his wars and give up their sovereignity. What would happen to the Hospitallers in the countries at war with the liege lord aided by the Hospitallers' headquarters? Wisely the order did not accept any offer, until they had a guarantee that they could remain sovereign. Their choice of Malta cost them enormous sums but they won their political goals, at least for some time. It is no coincidence that the property of the Templars was given to the Hospitallers. In the conflict between the military and the economic goal, the Hospitallers had stuck to the military, but the Templars to the economic, which cost them status and made them too tempting a prey.

Eventually we turn to the conflict between the basic goals of the feudal, Catholic society from which the orders once evolved and the particular goals of the orders. The feudal or more specifically the chivalric goals were expressed in the vows of the knights: obedience, poverty and chastity. The general religious goals could be reduced to one single point: obedience to the pope.

The discipline of the military orders was considered extraordinary rigid. They asked for and generally got blind obedience. There are just a few flaws, such as a conflict between the last Grand Master of the Templars, James de Molay, and his Treasurer of the Templar, Hugh de Peraud, who gave harmful evidence against the order at the trial in Paris (Edith Simon: *The Piebald Standard*. Little, Brown, Boston 1959, pp. 232, 260, 270, 289, 291, 337). The breakdown of discipline in the defense of Malta, when the French conquered it in 1798 is a better case and probably seriously hurt the reputation of the Hospitallers.

Poverty of the members could of course be combined with luxury of the order. The knights were fighting men needing their full strength and so forbidden excessive fasting, etc. The accusation of luxurious living seems not to have been taken seriously by anybody, but possibly in the last period of the Hospitallers' reign in Malta, when it meant very little for their reputation. Even so, the knights as individuals evidently kept their promise of poverty.

What about their promise of chastity? They were accused of homosexuality, which would be easy to practice in the orders with their stress on blind obedience. Homosexuality was not uncommon in the nobility at this time and some cases probably occurred in the orders too, but hardly to a large extent. Heterosexual contacts are rarely mentioned, still more rarely proved. There was a saying in Cyprus, that a lady who had not had a Templar as a lover, did not know her way around. The knights of Malta are said to have had mistresses. The outsider's impression is that the members of the military orders kept their three vows. The exceptions were few as long as the orders still fought in the Holy Land.

Then there are their religious duties and faith. The Templars were accused of idolatry, and some historians consider that at least some groups of them might have been guilty. Another accusation was that they had two initiations, the first good, but the second including profanation such as spitting and stamping on the cross. Several knights admitted themselves guilty, but the confessions were obtained under torture or under threats of torture. At the trial in Paris (1309—1310) nearly all of the imprisoned Templars repudiated their earlier confessions. The inquisition in France was, however, efficient enough to secure some points that could be used against the Templars.

The Teutonic knights make a far better case for heresy. During the reformation the knights in Prussia and in Livonia, with few exceptions, accepted the Lutheran faith of their Brandenburg neighbors, and in the same way the balli of Utrecht in Netherlands accepted Calvinism, as the rest of the country. The bond between the pope and the military orders had been strong. In one sense the orders represented the only fighting forces the pope could use in defense of Catholicism and accordingly the popes protected the military orders against ambitious monarchs. When the reformation gave some monarchs a free hand to take over the possessions of the church, they included the properties of the orders and they did not respect them outside their own territories either. Once the reformation had won over the majority of the Teutonic knights, the pope had, however, no reason to protect them, on the contrary, they should have been tried before an ecclesiastical court for heresy. There was little else for the knights to do, but to transform their lands into the two duchies of Prussia and of Courland. The priory of Hospitallers in Brandenburg accepted Lutheranism, stayed in the country keeping their possessions and in 1763 began paying responsions to Malta again. Their property was taken over in 1810 by the the impoverished Prussian Crown.

We have thus found that the goals of the military orders sometimes did come in conflict with one another. The military goal of the Hospitallers certainly came to dominate their hospitality goal, but the hospitals of Malta had a good reputation until their very last (Edgar E. Hume: *Medical Work of the Knights Hospitallers of St. John of Jerusalem*. John Hopkins Press 1940, p. 201). The interaction between military, economic and political goals is of course very complicated, but generally war and politics are easier to combine with each other than with economic strength as wars and allies both have to be paid. As the new national states in Europe arose, the fighting power of the orders meant less and less and so their political power decreased too. Their economic resources were reduced first by the reformation, then by the French revolution. Formally the order of St. John still is sovereign, still has ambassadors etc., but its political strength is gone, so is its military. The order has some property, officially to be used for the only original goal left to them: caring for the sick and the wounded. But of course new goals might have succeeded the old ones.

The Religious Orders of Knighthood in Our Time

The military orders built their existence on the ideologies of chivalry, feudalism and Catholicism. When these changed or disappeared, the orders had to change too. Their original set of goals: hospitality, military, economic and political strength, were increasingly difficult to realize. Some shadow of sovereignty still clung to Hospitallers and Teutonic knights as the Grand Master and the German Master remained princes of their domains in Germany until 1809. How could they keep up appearance? How have they been able to survive to these very days?

Those questions are not unambiguous and could be answered in many ways. We could tell in detail what happened to them. We could give examples of good men and wise decisions increasing their vitality and prestige. But we prefer to go on the way we have started, that is, to associate them with the Catholic ideology and to point out their new goals.

The Catholic Church has been able to blend new elements and old. The military orders certainly belong to the old, just like the other religious orders. And the pope still has the power to secure the survival of a military order by transforming it into an exclusively religious order, such as the modern Teutonic order. The order of St. Maurice and St. Lazarus in a similar way has been changed to a charitable organization.

Examples as these make the sociologists curious. Why take the trouble to dissolve or transform these organizations if they have no property and no power, only a dead tradition behind them? Well, they are paid the compliment to be handled as if they had resources and this belief has to be taken seriously, as it influences actions and thus has consequences which are real. What kind of goals could we then assign them, goals different from the original set, purified from political ambitions, meaningless and yet respected or even feared. Well, one goal is easy to point out: the order and its perpetuation is a goal in itself. To keep it alive, the leaders are willing to give up nearly everything, to accept nearly anything; symbols as standards, insignia, archives, registers and an old treasure chest might mean more to them than the content of that chest. We realize, however, that this new goal of the surviving orders is little more than a rephrasing of the fact that they have survived. Well, some of them did, some of them did not. Which survived? From the sociologist's point of view the answer is given. Survival is easier if the order is spread over large territories. Fame or high status is also important, attracting attention and eager recruits.

If we insert status as a goal, we can easily rephrase other difficult points too. It is important to suppress an order if its members are to be deprived status. It is important to reorganize or transform it, if other groups are to be given the status of the former set. It is important for the status of an order to get status from high status members in order to be able to give some status to the low status members. And high status in our days no longer means high nobility. The orders have to accept high status of several kinds if they are to keep their status: not only high officers, courtiers and clergy but also eminent men from civil services, law, industry and commerce. The status of scientists and artists seems to be used very reluctantly by

The Religious Orders of Knighthood

the high status orders, possibly indicating that science and art still have little status outside their own domains. The techniques to open the old orders to prominent men with new kinds of status is old and venerable too. We give three examples.

First, the Hospitallers' hospitals were used by *donats* who paid a sum for their maintenance. They were laymen, but associated with the order. This category could be used for status purposes, giving good candidates, who paid the donat sum, the insignia of the order, slightly changed to show the experts that these donats did not possess the status of a knight; but still, they *did* belong to an order of high status and got some status without declassing the class of fullfledged knights too much. The donats were many in the Austrian-Bohemian Grand Priory of the Hospitallers. The Teutonic order, then seated in Vienna, in 1871 added a similar class, the cross of Mary (Marianerkreuz), to their organization.

The second technique, used by the Hospitallers, also went back to the times of the crusaders. Influential candidates to the order, royal bastards, etc., who did not pass the rigorous tests for noble birth and legitimacy a number of generations back, sometimes were able to contrive papal permission to enter the order by papal grace and later by the grace of the order itself. They were classified as "Knights by grace", distinguished from the knights by justice and to the expert eye there were some small differences in the insignia, thus making it possible for the knights by justice to keep their self esteem intact while the order could use the initiation fee and outside citizen status of the non noble new knights to build up resources and some status for the order itself. The last steps in their democratization of the most feudal organizations still in existence were to open the Grand cross class to knights by honor and knights by grace. The third technique tried by the order of St. John was to use its sovereignity to institute an order of merit quite for itself to reward services to itself just as nearly all other states have.

To the sociologist the original goal of the military orders was to take care of pilgrims and sick. It was soon supplemented with the goals of military, economic and political strength and when these additional goals no longer could be realized in modern Europe, the orders still clung to an official goal of hospitality and so were enabled to make their organization and its survival to their real goal, using the status their traditions, their insignia and their similarity to the modern orders of merit brought them, to attract some high status members, who indirectly could help the order to give some extra status to acceptable candidates asking for it. And of course this is exactly the kind of hospitality and care many men in Western society badly need. In that sense the orders have remained faithful to their first goal.

Chapter 3
The Sodalities and Their Transformation into Orders

The legends about Charlemagne surrounded by his faithful heroes and Arthur with his knights of the round table not only gave rise to a litterature in the age of chivalry but also formed a part of the ideology. Then Templars and Hospitallers were to be found at all European courts, valiant men and trustworthy as far as their vows and their steady loyalty to the pope allowed them. It is easy to understand the medieval prince, eager for everlasting fame among the minstrels, who tried to form round him a circle of devoted and mighty knights, capable of great deeds, by creating not an order—only the pope could do that—but a sodality, binding with solemn vows to his person and his house the most prominent nobles and most valiant knights among his vassals, giving them the golden chains and the insignia of his sodality as a sign of his friendship and trust in them. Their vow was a vow of fidelity to him. Chastity and poverty made no sense here. The loyalty thus expected also meant, that no member of one sodality could accept the membership of another sodality. Still, the loyalty of the high and mighty to their liege lord and his sodality only too often proved to be far frailer than the loyalty of Hospitallers, Templars and Teutonic knights to the pope and their order.

Many sodalities disappeared just as fast as they had been created. It is often difficult to see whether the prince had meant only to create a number of knights using a more solemn ceremonial than usual or to initiate a sodality to serve his house for the future. Some orders later were introduced as "revivals" of early sodalities or dubbing of knights, which was a convenient way to invest them with more status and tradition.

The term sodality is now obsolete. We use it here in order to stress the difference between on one hand the military religious orders acknowledged by the pope, on the other hand the secular sodalities created by princes, and using the title of knight, the accolade and the golden chain of the knight, with a "jewel", that is, a golden pendant symbolizing the order or its saint patron. The simplest way to present the sodalities is to describe a number of the most well known. The sodalities surviving the French revolution all gradually changed into orders in the modern sense of the word.

The Garter

Froissart says in his Chronicle *(The Chronicles of England, France and Spain,* Dutton, New York, 1961, p. 37): "Edward on his return to England resolved to rebuild and embellish the great castle of Windsor, which king Alfred had founded, and where he had established that round table whence so many knights had issued forth, and displayed their prowess over the whole world. He further desired to institute an order of knighthood, to be denominated "Knights of the Blue Garter"; the knights were to be forty in number, and according to report and estimation, the bravest men in Christendom; at this time also he founded Windsor Chapel, and appointed canons there to serve God. The feast of the order of knights of the Blue Garter was to be celebrated at Windsor every year, on St. George's day."

Froissart lived in England as Secretary to king Edward's queen, Philippa. Still, he seems to be wrong in two things. The order of Garter can not have been created in 1344 as he suggests, as the Black Prince, one of the first members of the order, was not dubbed a knight until 1346, and only knights could be initiated to the order. The order, however, must have existed in 1348. The second mistake of Froissart is the number of knights. They were probably only twenty-five with the king.

There is no good explanation for the choice of St. George to patron of the order. St. George was believed to have been a Cappadocian knight, raised to a high command by the heathen emperor Diocletianus, whom he reproached for persecuting the Christians. This made him a martyr the 23rd of April in 290. His grave was shown at Lydda near Jaffa. His dragon he probably had taken over from the tale of Perseus and Andromeda. Richard Coeur-de-Lion won a battle against Saladin in 1192, the 23rd of April at Jaffna, near Lydda and this might have been a point in the favor of the saint. King Edward I always used the badge of St. George—red cross in white field, like that of the Templars. The Englishmen fighting the French in the fourteenth century used the cross of St. George on their coats, and "Saint George for England" as their battle cry.

The Garter's blue and golden colors are the royal French colors and could proclaim Edward's aspirations on the French crown.

The garter alone was the sign worn by the chosen knights. King Henry VII instituted the collar and the badge, now called 'the George', as it depicts St. George on horseback with his spear in the heart of the dragon.

The order of the Garter is one of the first sodalities and one of the few surviving in our days. The change into a state order came slowly, but when Henry V gave the kings of Denmark, Spain and Portugal the Garter, it can no longer be considered a sodality.

The French Order of the Star

The Garter is said to have impressed King John II of France deeply. He founded with pomp and circumstance the order of the Star, to be the French counterpart of the Garter (in 1351). In the war between England and France the Black Prince with a small but excellent army retreated from John's troops and was forced to fight at Poitiers (in 1356). John's army was badly mauled, many of his knights killed and he himself taken prisoner. The order of the Star was extinguished.

The fame of the order thus did not last long, but King John certainly chose a good name for it. Many orders, also new ones, use the star for their name and/or their insignia.

The Order of the Collar, or of Annunziata

As usual little is known about the foundation of the order, only the year and some of the first members. The founder, Amadeus VI, count of Savoy, was also "the true founder of the greatness of Savoy" (*Cambridge Medieval History,* vol. VII. Cambridge 1932. p. 59). Ambitious and successful politician on a large scale, he took the cross in 1363 and made a brilliant crusade of his own against Turks and Bulgars in 1366. His sodality of the Collar probably was meant to ease this well planned campaign (Aziz Atiya: *The Crusades in the Later Middle Ages,* 2nd ed. New York, 1965, p. 384).

The order of the Collar may have given some status to count Amadeus, but it certainly also gained status with him and with the rise of his house of Savoy, which obtained ducal rank from the Roman emperor in 1416. The order was meant to be a sodality, but the house of Savoy soon used it in their complicated and ruthless political game and so turned it into an order. Duke Charles III in 1518 changed its name to Annunziata and gave the pendant a form corresponding to the new name. When the house of Savoy succeeded to unite all Italian states to a kingdom, the order of Annunziata was made the highest ranking decoration of Italy. It survived until the end of World War II.

The Hungarian Order of the Dragon

Sigismund of the Luxemburg dynasty married the Hungarian queen Mary in 1385 and so obtained the throne of Hungary. His father, emperor Charles IV, gave him only Brandenburg, but he himself was elected German king in 1411, inherited the title king of Bohemia in 1419, was elected Lombard king in 1431 and Roman emperor in 1433. He lived abroad for long periods and the Hungarian lords grew in power. His sodality of the Dragon, founded in 1408, may have been a device to win loyalty and obedience from his status seeking and ambitious magnates. The house of Luxemburg lost its influence in the end of the 15th century and the order of the Dragon seems to have extinguished before 1500. The Habsburg dynasty claimed the Hungarian crown since 1526, but most of the country for a long time was in Turkish hands. The Habsburg family already possessed the order of the Golden Fleece and so had no use for the Hungarian Dragon.

The order of St. Hubert in the Duchy of Bar

Duke Louis of Bar in 1416 founded the Order of St. Hubert. Louis was a younger son, bishop of Chalons and a cardinal, when his elder brother Edward together with a third brother and a nephew was killed at Agincourt in 1415. Duke Louis seems to have been a pious man, at least he used his new sodality for the best of his duchy to recognize and reward those nobles of his country who had showed exceptional charity to the church or the poor. This restriction gave the order little fame. The duchy of Bar—and its sodality—was united with Lorraine. The former Polish king Stanislaw Leszczynski was granted Lorraine in 1738. When he died in 1766, duchy and order passed to the French kings. St. Hubert was officially made a royal

French order in 1786. The revolution suppressed it, but Louis XVIII revived it in 1816. It was finally abolished in 1824. The sodality has nothing more in common with the Bavarian order of St. Hubert than the patron giving them the same name.

The Order of the Golden Fleece

Philip the Good, duke of Burgundy, founded this famous order at his marriage to Isabella of Portugal in 1429 at Bruges to honor his bride. Philip stated "that his object was to honour worthy knights and to encourage feats of chivalry, for the reverence of God, the maintenance of the Christian faith, and the honour of knighthood." Some of the rules of the Order were well calculated to excite knightly ardour, but some clearly inculcated loyalty to the duke and his house. Each knight swore on his election to render personal service if anyone tried to damage the duke or his successors, to submit all quarrels between himself and other members of the order to the arbitration of the duke or his deputy, and not to undertake wars or long journeys without his license. To keep up a standard of conduct worthy of the Order, a stringent examination into the behavior of each knight was made at meetings of the chapter, and they were all required to give information about their fellows. Any knight guilty of heresy, treason or flight from the battle field, was expelled from the Order; for less serious offences lighter punishments were inflicted." (*Cambridge Medieval History* Vol. VI, Cambridge 1929, p. 810.)

The first chapter of the order was held at Lille in 1431, but in 1432 Dijon, the capital of Burgundy, was made its seat. The number of knights was two dozen, the Grand Master included, but like all these sodalities, the number was increased, first to 31, then to 51.

The son of Philip the Good, Charles the Bold, tried to unite Netherlands, Burgundy and Luxemburg with the countries between them to a kingdom of his own. He and his dream with him died at the battle outside Nancy in 1477. The same year his daughter Mary married the Austrian archduke Maximilian and thus the Burgundian heritage, including the order of the Golden Fleece, went to the house of Habsburg. Emperor Charles V was Grand Master of the order and left the grand mastership to his son, King Philip II of Spain, and the order then remained in Spain until the extinction of the Habsburg house there in 1700. The war of the Spanish succession (1701—13) ended with a partition of the Spanish heritage. The order of the

Golden Fleece was not mentioned in the treaties and so the new Bourbon dynasty in Spain created their knights of the Golden Fleece while the Habsburg dynasty in Vienna created theirs. The order thus was divided into two, showing that at this time the former sodality was a state order, belonging to the crown of Spain just as much as to the house of the founder and his successors, that is, the dynasty of Habsburg.

The Austrian order lasted until the fall of the Habsburgs in 1918, the Spanish until 1930. Franco, however, restored the order but no new knights have been created.

The Order of St. Maurice in Savoy

Amadeus VIII, the first duke of Savoy, retired from his reign in 1434 and created the order of St. Maurice in the same year for his circle of friends. The members were few, six or seven. They reserved two days a week for religious exercise and five for secular purposes. Amadeus accepted, however, the role of antipope, under the name of Felix V. This step made the order fall in abeyance to 1572, when duke Charles Emanuel of Savoy asked the pope to revive it as an order fighting for the Catholic faith. The pope did so on the conditions that it was united with the order of Lazarus and the Grand Mastership vested in the crown of Savoy. The order then grew in importance with the house of Savoy. King Victor Emanuel of Sardinia reorganized the order in 1816. When the house of Savoy succeeded in uniting the Italian states to the kingdom of Italy, the order of St. Maurice and St. Lazarus was organized in five classes and given the traditional organization of a state order. After World War II it was transformed into a charitable organization.

The Order of St. Mark in Venice

Very little is known about this order, but probably it was instituted during the 15th century.

The Order of the Elephant and of the Arm in Armour

The Danish kings seem to have created several sodalities, and the elephant was used as a symbol of a Danish sodality already in 1508. King Frederick II used a badge of a golden elephant for a sodality of his own in 1580. The order of the Arm in Armour was instituted in 1616, but passed out in 1634 or was united with the order of the Elephant. King Christian V gave the first statutes to this later order in 1693. The Garter in England and the Elephant in Denmark thus are the only sodalities still in existence. The order of the Elephant is the highest order in Denmark and is given only to heads of states and a small number of eminent Danes.

The Order of St. Hubert in Jülich and in Bavaria

Duke Gerard V of Jülich and Berg won an important battle on St. Hubert's day at Ravenburg in 1444 and so chose St. Hubert as the patron of his new sodality, founded in the same year. The heritage of Jülich passed to the Palatinate and in 1708 the elector John William found it useful to revive the order. When the Bavarian branch of the house of Wittelsbach extinguished in 1777, the two countries were united. The order of St. Hubert was given new statutes in 1803, still had only one class and remained reserved for roman Catholics, crowned heads, eminent statesmen and high nobility. When the Wittelsbach dynasty ended their reign in 1918, the order was dissolved.

The Order of St. Michael and the Order of the Holy Ghost in France

Among the first knights of the Garter were three Frenchmen, in the future loyal to Edward III. This might have been a reason for King John to create his Order of the Star. In the same way the fame of the Golden Fleece in Burgundy might have made the French King Louis XI anxious to counteract its influence by a sodality of his own, St. Michael, founded in 1469. The number of knights was originally low, but the French dynasty was hard pressed and had to use all its resources. The actual number of knights soon was far above the stipulated and the status of the order thus decreased, although a number of sovereigns belonged to the order. King Henry III then in 1578 created a new order, of the Holy Ghost, and got rid of his old sodality, by uniting them, the averse side of the cross showing a dove, symbolizing the Holy Ghost, while the reverse showed St. Michael.

This order of the Holy Ghost certainly did acquire status of fame. The cross was born either in a chain or in a light blue ribbon. Ribbons more and more replaced the heavy collars or chains of the sodalities—at least in every day life and for less important occasions—and then the light blue color had taken over some of the status of the order itself. Light blue ribbons thus were chosen for the Garter, the Annunziata (only for officials having no collar), the Elephant, the Order of St. Andrew in Russia, of the White Eagle in Poland, of the Seraphim in Sweden, all of them in one class, all of them the highest order of the country, reserved for a limited number of princes and very high officials.

The order of the Holy Ghost was dissolved during the French revolution. The Bourbons returned to France and when the orders were revived, King Louis XVIII separated the two orders again, the order of the Holy Ghost keeping its light blue ribbon, its exclusivity and high status, the order of St. Michael given a black ribbon, a less important purpose: to reward merits in Art or Science, and a less restricted membership, as there were to be one hundred knights.

The two revived orders did not survive very long, as both of them were abolished after the revolution in 1830.

The Sociologist's Points of View

When we try to summarize what sodalities have in common, we cannot tell anything new to the historians. We only apply another set of concepts, some of which may sound a bit strange or barbaric.

Sodalities were originally created only by a liege lord for his vassals in order to attatch them to his cause, his person or his house. They generally were founded in a particular political situation to promote the more or less open political program of the founder. Coronations, marriages and military campaigns formed important and quite impressive parts of such programs and so they often were used to motivate a new and useful sodality. But most sodalities lived no longer than the particular political constellation they were adapted for. The founder forgot his sodality the moment he no longer had use for it.

A sodality had a greater chance to survive in a stable political climate, with a strong tradition behind it—if the members in their own right had very high status in the state. Such a sodality was really a good instrument in the sovereign's hand to be handled as a highly useful reward of loyalty and merit—and also to create loyalty within the sodality. But such a sodality was far to important to be respected as personal property of a prince or his house. It belonged to his country and if a usurper succeeded to take the throne, he also took the sodality, cast out those members, whom he did not appreciate, and so could appoint some new knights loyal to himself. Henry VII, of England is a good case. He was not a member of the Garter himself, but very soon got rid of the knigths in some sense loyal to the lost case of York.

The sodality of course acquired status from its members. If the prince made only the most powerful lords member of his sodality, it gave status to the sodality, but need not give it stability or loyalty. Great lords had great aims and ambitions. They were used to break vows and alliances when they had to. The vows of loyalty thus meant less, the more status they already possessed. But if their policy had to be secret, the more important was the friendship and the membership in the sodality of the prince they meant to destroy. The more complicated the political situation the more difficult to see the difference between friends and foes, the more important to use the control the sodality could give: the members had to come to the chapter of the order, had to defend their personal acts, were forbidden long journeys unless the monarch gave them leave, had to take their quarrels to the prince and accept his decision, etc.

The sodalities thus were important from the political point of view, but also from the economic. To be initiated in the leading sodality was a very high compliment—and it cost the monarch very little. Embassies going abroad could bring the insignia of a sodality instead of costly gifts, etc. This of course undermined the political use of the sodalities. Or we might say, that when powerful monarchs had established centralized states, they no longer needed sodalities for the political control of the country; they used them instead as rewards dear to the new member, but cheap to the state.

Thus the change of the sodality into an order of the state was completed and the main question was what scale should be used. How many knights were to be made happy? Few knights meant a high gratification but to few, many knights meant less gratification to many. The monarchs soon learned how to balance this. They also learned to offer and to accept the orders of one another, to keep the number down all the same by keeping foreigners outside the "real" number of knights and, eventually, to allow their subjects to accept orders from abroad although this in principle, but now only in principle, meant a break in loyalty toward the liege lord.

The sociologist thus can point out some goals of the sodalities:

1. Loyalty to a) the prince b) his house c) his country
2. Status to a) the prince b) his house c) his country
3. Status to the member. He often had the right to call his monarch cousin etc.
4. Creating contacts. Membership could be restricted to few or extended to many.

These four goals generally tend to counteract one another, although exceptions might be common. We could argue like this:

1. Loyalty to a prince should be greater the lower status the new member had before, that is, the less status he can give the prince etc. (2), but if the sodality did not get status from most of its members, it could not give much status to those who had little status previously. (3). The loyalty to the prince eventually was larger, the more he restricted the number of knights in his sodality (4),

2. A prince acquired more status from his sodality if he chose the greatest lords to his sodality, but this then meant comparatively little to them (3) and he had to restrict the number of the members (4),

3. The members acquire more status from a sodality, the more restricted it is.

These three points thus indicate that the goals of the sodalities tended to collide.

The general tendencies we discussed, are easy to circumvent in a number of cases. The monarch could for instance mix the membership in his sodality or order, take some of them from the great lords and some from the most eminent of his officials outside the nobility, thus using the sodality to transmit some of the nobility halo to his loyal helpers of lower origin, etc, etc. We suspect, however, that the goals we sketched above in practice did counteract one another.

The goal of loyalty probably was the most important, when the sodalities flowered. As the monarchs in the centralized states succeeded in concentrating the power in their hands, loyalty was secured, anyhow, and so was the status of the monarch and his house. Then the surviving sodalities could be used to give status to the members. The king of course more or less reserved the status of his order to those of the nobility who had had to give up most power to him and so should be given consolation and status, that did not cost too much and in reality meant very little. The sodalities, however, by definition must restrict their contact net. And so the orders of the state present a better solution when the need to expand the contact net grew.

This goal analysis might have been of some interest, if the princes handling their sodalities had been aware of the conflicting goals, because then their decisions about sodalities would say something important about the political situation then and there as they saw it. But the change of the sodalities into state orders still has some interest as it is an easily accessible aspect on the transformation of feudal countries into centralized monarchies.

Chapter 4
The Emergence of the State
Orders of Knighthood
(until 1700)

At the middle of the 16th century all the surviving military orders had accepted the monarch as Grand Master, placed their resources at his disposal and their members were appointed by him. The only exceptions were the order of St. John (at Malta) and the Teutonic knights surviving at Mergentheim. The sodalities represented quite another tradition, other vows, other ceremonies and other goals, still, at this time military orders as well as sodalities in our opinion were used by the monarch just to manipulate status relations, using traditions, ceremonies and insignia to impress their political allies abroad and their prominent subjects at home with an act of grace that cost little and gave no real power. Then we have no reason to keep orders and sodalities apart any longer. They were both used the same way, although the Catholic monarchs generally were more inclined to organize their new orders along the lines of the military order while the Protestant monarchs preferred the sodality pattern: only one class and no religious vows of any kind.

We try to demonstrate this point by presenting first five Catholic orders: St. Stephen in Tuscany, the Papal order of the Golden Spur, the Bavarian orders of St. George and of St. Michael and Constantines order of St. George in Parma, then three Protestant orders: The order of Generosity in Brandenburg; the order of Dannebrog in Denmark, the order of the Thistle in Scotland and England and eventually the Russian order of St. Andrew.

The Order of St. Stephen in Tuscany

The Medici family in Florence was expelled in 1527, but the city surrendered in 1530 to the troops of emperor Charles V and then the Medicis returned. Duke Alessandro, murdered in 1537, was followed by Cosimo, who created the order of St. Stephen in 1554 and was made a Grand duke of Tuscany in 1569. The peace of Cateau-Cambrisis in 1559 gave a period of rest to Italy, used well by Cosimo who succeeded to aggrandize Tuscany in many ways. His new state had, however, no fleet and the coasts often were plundered by Turkish pirates. His new order he made a naval one. The knights made a vow to fight the infidels. The order was confined to the nobility, and was intended to interest them in State service, to attatch them to the dynasty, to wean them away from faction and the pursuit of wealth. The knights were endowed with Commanderies founded by the State or by wealthy private families. They won distinction at Penon de Velez in 1564, and at Lepanto in 1571. But the little fleet never reached its intended number of twenty galleys, and could scarcely keep the sea when the Barbaresques appeared in force. On the other hand it paid its way, for Cosimo used it for his private commerce. (*Cambridge Modern History.* Vol. III, p. 391). Here fighting infidels still was a goal, after all.

The order of St. Stephen was revived in 1817 by the Grand Duke Ferdinand III, but then only as a state order and divided in four classes. When Tuscany was made part of Italy in 1859, the order was not dissolved but no new members appointed.

The Papal Order of the Golden Spur (Miliza Aurata)

The pope seems to have created this order in the 16th century out of an earlier knightly organization and probably hoped to use it for military purposes, as Cosimo was able to use his order of St. Stephen. This goal may have influenced pope Pius IV:s decision in 1559 to delegate to some members of his court and to a number of noble families in Rome the right to appoint members. The order never could be used for military purposes, and the number of knights soon robbed it of all status, although Mozart, however, was made a knight of the order.

Pope Gregory XV in 1841 abolished the order, uniting it with his new order of St. Sylvester and placed a little golden spur on the insignia of St. Sylvester as a token of its old tradition. But in 1905 pope Pius X needed a new order and then separated the two orders again, taking the spur off the insignia of the order of St. Sylvester and giving an impressive exterior to his new order of the Golden Spur, which he used as a distinction for foreign heads of state and eminent statemen.

The Bavarian Orders of St. George and of St. Michael

The order of St. George was instituted by the elector Maximilian Emanuel, probably at the begin of the long campaign against the Turks, that started in 1683, and still had some similarity to a crusade. The statutes of the order was under these circumstances of less importance than the knights and Max Emanuel never bothered himself with the formal statutes. They were given by his son Ferdinand Maria.

If there originally was a military goal for the order, it was forgotten after the Turkish wars. The electors used their order to reward the high nobility, and in 1778 the order was divided in one division for dignitaries of the Catholic church and another for secular nobility, both divisions in three classes: grand crosses, commanders (or priors), knights or chaplains. The order was abolished when the Wittelsbach dynasty ended its reign of Bavaria in 1918.

The order of St. Michael was instituted in 1693 as a "House order of knights" by the elector Maximilian Emanuel, when he had been made governor of the Spanish Netherlands in 1691 as a reward for his services in the wars against Turkey and France. He was married to the Austrian archduchess Maria Antonia, daughter of emperor Leopold I and the Spanish infanta Margaret, which gave him hopes that his son Joseph Ferdinand should inherit the Spanish crown after the childless Charles II. The elector manipulated the Spanish Netherlands and Bavaria for this purpose and the order of St. Michael may have been part of his manipulations. They were useless, however, as Joseph Ferdinand died in 1699. The order of St. Michael seems to have had little status and was reorganized in 1721.

When the Wittelsbach line in the Palatinate inherited Bavaria in 1777, they brought with them the order of St. Hubert and made it the highest ranking order of Bavaria. They then in 1778 gave the order of St. George three classes instead of one and so could use it to acquire loyalty from and give status to a larger number of the Bavarian Catholic nobility. In the same way they also used the order of St. Michael, ranking third on their scale, as a reward for a less restricted set of subjects. St. Michael thus got three classes in 1837, five classes in 1855 and six in 1910. Both orders were abolished in 1918.

Constantine's Order of St. George in Parma and Naples

Among the Greeks fleeing from Constantinople to Italy was a member of the imperial house of the Paleologii, John Angelus, who accepted the hospitality of the Farnese family in Parma. He gave himself out as the hereditary Grand master of a Greek order of knighthood, founded by the emperor Constantine and dedicated to St. George. When he died childless, he is said to have given the order to the house of Farnese. Francis I, duke of Parma, revived the order in 1698 and made himself Grand master. The order seems to have been handled skillfully as it had high status. The last of the Farnese family died in 1731. The duchy of Parma—and Constantine's order of St. George—passed to duke Charles of Bourbon, who in 1735 made himself king of Naples and brought the order with him there. He was replaced in Parma by his brother, duke Philip, who also had need of the order and so kept it. There were thus two orders of St. George with the same origin but in different countries, just as there were two orders of the Golden Fleece, one in Austria and one in Spain.

The Napoleonic time in Italy made an end of the Parmesan order in 1806, but when the duchy of Parma was reestablished in 1814, so was the order of Constantine. It then had four classes: grand crosses, commanders, knights by justice and knights by grace. The duchy of Parma was made a part of Italy in 1860, but the order is said to survive as a religious order.

The kingdom of Naples was conquered by the French and king Ferdinand fled to Sicily protected by Nelson's fleet. Napoleon gave the kingdom of Naples first to his brother Joseph, then to his brother in law Joachim Murat, who succeeded to save his kingdom in 1814, but joined Napoleon during his 100 days and so ended his days in front of an execution squad. King Ferdinand returned to his kingdom, renamed it the Two Sicilies and also brought his orders back with him. The Two Sicilies were made a part of Italy in 1860 and then the order of St. George was abolished as an secular order of knighthood.

The Order of Generosity in Brandenburg

During the reign of the Great elector in Brandenburg, one of his older sons in 1667 founded a sodality for his friends and named it l'Ordre de la Générosité. It had only one class and thus can be considered a typical sodality at the start. It survived as such to 1740, when Frederick the great either reorganized it as the order of Merit (Pour le Mérite) or the new order superseded the old. It still had only one class and was used to reward military or civil merit. During the Napoleonic wars the order was reorganized in 1810 exclusively for military merit. A civil division with special insignia was created in 1842 to reward merits in arts and sciences. The military division had a very high reputation and in 1866, a military grand cross class was added to it. The military division was abolished in 1918.

The civil division was, however, reorganized in 1924 and then in 1958. It is still in existence.

The Danish Order of Dannebrog

King Christian V of Denmark came to the throne in 1670. His father had in 1665 made Denmark an absolute monarchy and broken the power of the nobility. The new king certainly had use for an order of knighthood to reward his nobility and his new high officials, most of them burghers. The first knights of the order were appointed in 1671. The statutes, however, were not given until in 1693. The order of Dannebrog thus was created at the same time as the order of the Elephant was reorganized, received statutes at the same time and was used very much the same way: as a sodality in one class to reward a very restricted group of high officials.

The order was reorganized in 1808 and divided in four classes, receiving more classes each following reorganization. It now has two classes of grand crosses, two classes of commanders, two classes of knights and one silver Cross of Honor.

The Most Ancient Order of the Thistle

James II founded the order in 1687 for the sovereign and only eight knights. He considered it a revival of an old Scottish order of knighthood, and dedicated it to St. Andrew. He certainly needed all loyalty that tradition and status could give a Catholic king in Presbyterian Scotland. The Glorious revolution in 1688 ended the reign of James II and could have ended the order of the Thistle too, unless queen Anne had not revived it in 1703 and appointed new knights. The number of knights then was 12 and in 1827 it was raised to 16. This order was thus constructed along the same lines as the Garter and seems to have been meant—and used—as the Scottish equivalent of the English Garter. This was evident also from the statute: if a knight of the Thistle was rewarded with the Garter, he had to resign from the order of the Thistle.

The Russian Order of St. Andrew

Czar Peter I visited incognito Great Britain during "the Grand Embassy" to Western Europe in 1697 and 1698. He probably received some knowledge at that time about the order of the Thistle and its insignia with the cross of St. Andrew. And St. Andrew happened to be patron of Russia as well as of Scotland. There could thus be some connection between the order of the Thistle and the Russian order of St. Andrew, created in 1698, when Peter had returned to Russia and suppressed the revolt of the Streltsy.

The order of St. Andrew had only one class, was reserved for a small number of eminent officials and used the light blue ribbon of Holy Ghost. It remained the first order of Russia until 1917, when the reign of the Romanow dynasty ended.

The Compromise between Different Traditions

We have described the orders of St. Stephen (Tuscany), the Golden Spur (Holy See), the Bavarian orders of St. George and of St. Michael and the Parmesan Order of St. George in order to demonstrate the tendency of the Catholic monarchs in the 18th century to give their orders traditions from the military orders of the crusades, requiring the knights to be of noble births and to give vows (often to fight the infidels, to defend the Christian faith, etc.). These orders often were divided in several classes: grand crosses, commanders, knights by justice, knights by grace etc., just as the Templars or Hospitallers. And these orders still forced their members to engage in the activity of the order at least with money. The status conferred had to be paid.

The Protestant or Greek Orthodox countries had little use for these traditions. Their orders stressed only the loyalty to the sovereign and his house. They had only one class of knights, like the sodalities. This type of orders proved very useful to reward the high officials necessary for the administration of the centralized monarchies. But when we consider here the new orders, created in the 17th century, we must point out, that although few military orders survived in the Protestant countries, a number of sodalities survived in the Catholic countries: The Golden Fleece in Austria, The Holy Ghost in France, the order of the Collar in Savoy etc., all of them just as useful in these countries as their counter parts in the Protestant countries, as they saved the sovereign land, money or power when he could confer just status created for this very purpose by the pompous ceremony of initiating a grateful candidate to the circle round the king, marked off by their titles and insignia.

This idea of course paid best when used for the top groups which otherwise would have been very expensive to reward with gifts of money, land or offices. The idea was, however, too good to stay reserved for them, but if used on a lower level it also must be used on a far larger scale if it should pay. Louis XIV in France solved this balance problem in 1693, when he created his Royal and Military Order of St. Louis.

France then fought the war of the Grand Alliance aganist Austria, Netherlands, England. Louis won several battles and certainly had good reasons to reward his marshals and his officers although his resources were reduced by the war. He used his new order for this purpose and gave it the three classes of the military orders (grand crosses, commanders and knights). He kept the condition of Catholic faith but otherwise restricted the vow to loyalty just to himself. There were thus no burdens, only the insignia to demonstrate the status of the happy recipient. The Grand crosses were few, had very high status, little less than that of Holy Ghost. The commanders after all were restricted in number, wore the same red ribbon and badge as the grand crosses and probably enjoyed high status, as not too many really knew the difference between commander and grand cross. The number of knights was unlimited but still rather small from the modern point of view. These knights belonged to the same order as the grand crosses and commander, were given the accolade, took part in the ceremonies etc. and so got a reasonable amount of status out of their knighthood.

The order of St. Louis thus looked like an old military order from the crusades, and so we had better specify similarities and differences between for instance the order of St. John of Jerusalem (Hospitallers) and the new order of Louis XIV:

Similarities:

A saint patron.

Ceremony of initiation

Hierarchy:

grand master, grand crosses, commanders and knights

Insignia

Status to the order formed a goal in itself.

Differences:

The military religious orders were international, the order of St. Louis exclusively French.

The goal of protecting pilgrims or citizens not relevant for Order of St. Louis

The goals of military, economic or political strength just as irrelevant

Vows of chastity, poverty and obediance in the order of St. Louis were substituted by vows of loyalty to the sovereign, his house and his religion.

The military order was an organization under papal protection, electing its grand master, forming units for everyday life and battle. The order of St. Louis was a formal organization, having little but the insignia in common. The grand master alone made all important decisions.

The goal of the order of St. Louis thus was only to give as much status as possible to as many members as possible at a low cost.

But the last point is not new to us. At the end of the first chapter we have already assumed that the Hospitallers changed their original goal of hospitality to pilgrims and sick into hospitality to acceptable candidates asking for extra status by initiation into the order. Are we not trying to say very much the same about the order of St. Louis and still give this order the credit for the first efficient drive toward this goal of producing and distributing as much status as possible to large numbers of worthy men? Yes, but please remember that we discussed in the end of the second chapter the situation of the Hospitallers in the 20th century and that the order of St. Louis was created in 1693, when the Hospitallers still were busy fortifying La Valetta, sending out ships and galleys to fight the infidels. The order of St.

Louis thus should be regarded as the invention, the Hospitallers' case as a late application.

From the sociologist's point of view Louis XIV gave a good solution to a difficult problem by just skipping the traditional points of goals, vows, social interaction within the orders and keeping only loyalty, formal hierarchy, insignia and some ceremonies as instruments for the application of status. And so we expect some more of the absolute monarchs to take over this new pattern. They did not. At least not for a long time. And this fact we interpret as a demonstration of the strength of the traditions still surrounding the orders, traditions now out of place but very strong all the same. The ideology of the enlightenment showed, however, little respect for traditions and enlightened monarchs had a more sophisticated view. The first orders using the pattern of St. Louis were the Swedish order of the Sword and order of the North Star, both of them instituted in 1748 and both with two classes: commanders and knights. But this belongs to the next chapter.

Chapter 5
The European Orders of
Knighthood 1701—1792

Up to now we have discussed twelve military religious orders of the crusades, thirteen sodalities, and eleven orders created in the 17th century, altogether thirty-six orders instituted during six centuries. That is a low number and it is low, because so many of them—especially sodalities—existed just for a short time, so short that even if some data about them have survived, it is difficult to say whether they should be considered sodalities or orders or just an extra ceremonial touch at coronations, etc.

After 1700 data survive more easily and the official archives have been careful to register statutes etc., which gives the impression that orders have been created at an increasing rate. We believe this to be true but evidently the point cannot be demonstrated. Still, if we restrict ourselves to a comparison between the 17th and the 18th centuries, the risks are considerably smaller. Then we find only five orders founded between 1600 and 1700 (two more Austrian orders for noble ladies, a type of orders we have not yet discussed), but thirty-two orders founded between 1701 and 1792 (and five more for noble ladies).

At the start of the 18th century the tradition of the sodality still dominated and so a number of state orders in one class are founded: Salzburg got its order of St. Rupert in 1701, Courland the order of Gratitude the same year, Württemberg the order of the Hunting Horn in 1702, Poland the White Eagle in 1705 and Brandenburg-Anspach its Ordre de la Sincereté in the same year, Prussia the Black Eagle in 1710, Baden the order of Fidelity in 1715, Russia Alexander Newski in 1725, Holstein-Gottorp St. Anne in 1735, Saxony St. Henry in 1736, Saxe-Weimar the White Falcon in 1738, and Naples St. Januarius in the same year, Sweden the order of the Seraphim in 1748, Saxe-Coburg-Saalfeld St. Joachim in 1755, Hohenlohe the order of Phoenix in 1757, Poland St. Stanislaus in 1765, Limburg the order of the Four Emperors in 1768, the Palatinate the order of the Lion and Württemberg the order of Military Merit in the same year, Hesse-Cassel the order of Military Merit in 1769 and the order of the Golden Lion in 1770. Eventually Poland, in 1792, before its second partition, got the order of Military Virtue. All these twenty-two orders were founded with only one class.

Let us then have a look at the orders for noble ladies. They started in the Catholic countries and so picked up traits resembling nun-orders with vows of chastity and piety. The Austrian dowager empress Eleonora in 1662 founded an order, the Slaves of Chastity, so devoted to religion and nobility that it seems to have passed out rather fast. Already in 1668 she founded the Noble Order of the Star cross. She possessed a relique, a splinter of the Holy cross, very dear to her. When parts of the castle in Vienna burned down in 1668, she took the loss of the relique very seriously and when it was recovered, unhurt, out of the ashes, she considered this a miracle and founded her order as a token of it in 1668. It was in existance until 1918 and as the stamps are intact, new copies in gilt silver and enamel still can be produced.

Such an order could be used by an empress or queen much the same way as the monarchs used their high orders in one class and so the pattern spread: Russia instituted the order of St. Catherine in 1714, Würzburg the order of St. Anne in the same year for unmarried noble ladies, who were made honarary members, when they married. Bavaria founded an order of St. Elizabeth in 1766 and the order of St. Anne in 1783, both along the sames lines as the Würzburg order, King Charles IV of Spain created in 1792 the order of Mary Louisa for his queen to reward piety and charity, if demonstrated by very noble ladies.

We now turn to the military orders. Some of the high orders in only one class were meant exclusively for officers of high command: St. Alexander Newski in Russia, St. Henry in Saxony, the orders of Military Merit in Württemburg and Hesse-Cassel, the order of Military Virtue in Poland, all of them probably influenced by the French order of St. Louis, although they missed the point of division in several classes. When the enlightened monarchs at last realized the use of more than one class, they very often started with an exclusively military order and then followed up with a civil order or an order, where civilians also could be initiated. Frederick I of Sweden in 1748 founded the military order of the Sword and the civilian order of the North Star, both in two classes. Elizabeth

Christine, empress of Austria founded the order of Elizabeth Theresia for retired high officers in 1750 and gave it three classes. Empress Mary Theresia during her long war with Frederick the Great instituted in 1757 her order of Mary Theresia for courage in battle, in three classes, according to the military rank of the hero. The corresponding civil order, St. Stephen, with three classes, came in 1764.

France already had St. Louis for the officers, but it was restricted to Catholics, and in 1759 King Louis XV in the seven years war against England and Prussia, founded the corresponding order of Military Merit, open to non-catholics and using the same three classes as St. Louis. There was, however, no French order in several classes open for civil servants and prominent members of the third estate (which might have been a mistake). Russia created in 1769 the order of St. George with four classes to reward courage in battle and in 1772 the order of St. Wladimir, with just as many classes, open both to civilians and officers. Spain possessed old military orders in many classes, but in 1771 Charles III created his order of Charles III in two classes also for civil merit. Eventually Gustavus III of Sweden in 1772 created the order of Wasa for civil merit in three classes.

The pattern of the order in several classes thus had been accepted by the great European powers and a few ambitious states of second or third rank had followed the lead. Some of them demonstrated the strength of the new pattern by adding one or two new classes to their old order in one class. Hohenlohe's order of the Phoenix and Brandenburg-Anspach's order of Sincerety might serve as examples, the latter taken over, together with the little state itself, by Prussia in 1792, renamed the order of the Red Eagle, and both its classes opened to civilians as well as officers. The officers, however, had the order Pour le Mérite reserved for themselves, as it was a reward for extreme courage in battle.

We have now discussed the European orders up to the year of 1792. All European monarchs and governments by this time knew very well how to use state orders and what patterns to take over, when they felt the need to do so.

Needs arose as the states lacked better means than orders to reward nobility for being born, great generals for their victories and ability to survive, eminent statesmen for successful handling of their monarchs and their colleagues, prominent citizens for service of any kind.

The Set of European Orders at the end of 1792, from the Sociologist's Point of View

Up to now we have tried to follow the rise of the European orders, their background, their organization and their goals. We have described or given names of seventy-four orders, although some of these had passed out long before 1792. The sociologist then is anxious to proceed to the situation at the end of 1792, and anxious to apply macro-sociological methods, that is, he wants to know how many orders and what kind of orders are in use in European countries of different types. And so we have to discuss in some detail how to calculate number of orders, how to classify them and then how to classify the European countries.

Number of orders should mean only orders used by the sovereign or the government of the country. Obsolete orders should not be included. In some cases it is difficult to know, when an order is obsolete. Take for instance the order of St. Joachim in Saxe-Coburg-Saalfeld. It was created in 1755, and certainly was obsolete in 1826 when the duchy was united with Saxe-Meiningen. Was it obsolete already in 1792? We have not been able to prove that and so have to register it for 1792.

We classify the orders in four classes: 1) High orders in only one class, 2) Military orders exclusively used to reward military merits, 3) Civil orders, rewarding also the merits of civilians, 4) Orders for ladies.

The European countries are difficult to classify and even to enumerate, because there were several hundred small German states, all of them under the authority of the Holy Roman Empire but still with the same amount of formal independence as Baden, Bavaria, Saxony or Württemberg.

Our main goal here is, however, to compare sets of data about the European states at chosen time intervals. Then it is important to us not to change the sample of states more than is necessary. We have chosen the year of 1792, because it still represented l'ancien régime, the old Europe. But on the other hand we do not want to bring in the enormous number of small German states, nearly all of which disappear in the Revolutionary wars or their aftermath in Vienna, as their disappearance later would disturb the comparisons. But we are unwilling to exclude those small states which had founded orders, as that would mean loss of information. We have then decided to include the following German states among our set of states in 1792:

1. The Holy Roman Empire, which in 1792 meant little more than Austria.
2. The kingdom of Prussia, parts of which belonged to Germany.
3. The secular electors: Bavaria, Hannover, Saxony.
4. The princes of Anhalt-Bernburg and Anhalt-Dessau-Köthen, the margrave of Baden, the duke of Brunswick, the counts of Hesse-Cassel, Hesse-Darmstadt and Hesse-Homburg, the princes of Hohenlohe, of Hohenzollern-Hechingen and of Hohenzollern-Sigmaringen, the duke of Holstein-Gottorp, the Grand Master of St. John of Jerusalem, the prince of Liechtenstein, the duke of Limburg, the prince of Lippe, the dukes of Mecklenburg-Schwerin and of Mecklenburg-Strelitz, the prince of Nassau, the duke of Oldenburg, the princes of Reuss and Reuss-Gera, the dukes of Saxe-Altenburg, of Saxe-Coburg-Gotha, of Saxe-Coburg-Saalfeld, of Saxe-Meiningen, of Saxe-Weimar, the archbishop of Salzburg, the princes of Schaumburg-Lippe, of Schwarzburg-Rudolstadt and of Schwarzburg-Sondershausen, the German Master of the Teutonic order, the prince of Waldeck, the duke of Württemburg and the bishop of Würzburg.
5. The free city of Frankfort, later transformed to a grand duchy.

The Italian states are less complicated, but we enumerate them all the same:

1. The kingdoms of Naples, of Sardinia and then the Holy See.
2. The Grand duchy of Tuscany, the duchies of Lucca, Modena, Parma, the principality of Monaco.
3. The republics of San Marino and Venice (not Genoa, as it neither possessed an order nor did survive the Napoleonic Wars). These states we classify in four different ways according to:
1. Religion. Catholic faith once was a necessary condition for the foundation of an order and it influenced deeply the pattern of the orders. The other religions are of less interest to us, as Protestants and Greek Orthodox lack the Catholic tradition. We thus divide our countries in two classes, Catholic and non-Catholic.
2. Political power. We divide our states in three groups: Great powers, powers of the middle range and small states. Our great powers are France, Germany (Austria), Great Britain, Prussia, Russia, Spain and Turkey. The powers of the middle range are

the remaining kingdoms, the German electorial states as Bavaria and Saxony and the republics of Netherlands, Switzerland and Venice. As small states we recognize six Italian, thirty-four German states (with the knights of St. John and the Teutonic order) Courland and Andorra.

3. Rank of Sovereign: emperor, king, elector, duke, etc. We then use five classes: 1) empires, at this time the Holy Roman Empire of the German Nation (Austria), Russia and then Turkey, whose sultan or Grand-Turk was outside the hierarchy but high enough to belong to this class. 2) The ten European kingdoms: Denmark, France, Great Britain, Naples, Poland, Portugal, Prussia, Sardinia, Spain, Sweden and the Holy See. 3) The three secular electorates Bavaria, Hannover and Saxony (the ecclesiastical electors disappeared in 1803 and so are excluded here, as we want to make comparisons with cross-sections at later years as easy as possible). 4) The remaining thirty-nine monarchies, styled duchies, princedoms, counties, etc. 5) The six republics: Andorra, Frankfort, Netherlands, San Marino, Switzerland and Venice.

4. Colonies. They meant so much for a country at this time, that we use the simple classification of 1) colonial powers: Denmark, France, Great Britain, Netherlands, Portugal, Spain and Sweden, and 2) the remaining states.

These classifications are bound up with a set of theoretical points, which we try to formulate as hypotheses.

We expect, that Catholic faith eases the survival of medieval military orders, as Protestant monarchs quickly dissolved the orders in their country in order to confiscate their property. Greek Orthodox countries seem to have had no medieval military orders and so the old orders and their traditions ought to give Catholic countries more surviving orders in 1792.

We further expect that countries with more political power have a more numerous nobility, larger armies, more officers, larger areas and populations, hierarchies of civil servants more varied and stronger than countries with less political power. All these factors create a need to reward the members of the higher classes in the military and the civil hierarchies and so the countries with more political power should tend to have more orders.

We combine these two expectations and first have a general view of how orders of knighthood had been accepted in different countries, according to their religious faith and their political power. We then get the following table:

Proportion of states having orders in 1792, according to power and religion of the states.

Religion	Great powers	Powers of middle range	Small states	Sum
Catholic	3/3	7/8	7/16	17/27
Non-Catholic	3/4	3/5	7/26	13/35
Sum	6/7	10/13	14/42	30/62

The data support our expectations: Catholic countries tend to have more orders than non-catholic and great powers have more orders than the small states. Our hypotheses are not rejected, at least not in this first test.

To pursue this examination we could anticipate that Catholic faith and political power are associated not only with a system of state orders operating in 1792, but also with the number of orders included in this system. We expect that there is a strong traditional factor operating in each order, to keep the number of members as low as possible and the status of the accepted candidates as high as possible. If the sovereign disregards this tradition, there is a risk that the old members lose more status, at least in their own eyes, than the new members win and so the order would produce a loss of total status instead of a gain. The sovereign then can circumvent this traditional factor within his orders by creating a new order free from the criticism of old members as long as the new order is placed below the old ones. The pressure of candidates for insignia and orders thus ought to show indirectly in the number of orders, which is a convenient measure to us, as we have no chance to measure the number

Mean number of orders in European states of 1792, according to religion and power.

Religion	Great powers	Powers of middle range	Small states
Catholic	7.3	2.8	0.5
Non-Catholic	3.0	1.4	0.3

of members. The mean number of orders in the states, classified according to their faith and power is given in the last table p. 67.

The table shows that states with more political power had more orders and that Catholic states had a higher mean than the non-catholic states of the same class. This table, however, gives only a weak support to the previous one as they both are heavily influenced by the states having no orders at all.

We proceed to the rank of the sovereign and calculate the means for each class, expecting the higher ranks to possess more orders:

Mean number of orders in European states of 1792, according to the rank of the sovereign.

Empires (Germany, Russia, Turkey)	mean 4.3 orders
Kingdoms (10 and the Holy See)	3.7 orders
Electorates (Bavaria, Hannover, Saxony)	2.0 orders
Duchies, princedoms, counties (39)	0.5 orders
Republics (Andorra, Frankfort, Netherlands, San Marino, Switzerland, Venice)	0.2 orders

The orders certainly are associated with the rank of the sovereign. The republics have just one (and a doubtful one, the order of St. Mark in Venice) and so, very properly, from the sociological point of view, end at the bottom of our list.

There is no reason to associate orders with colonies, but indirectly, as colonies generally needed to be backed up by a powerful sovereign and also could add to his power. All of the colonial powers belonged to the more important states. It is of little value to compare them with states lacking colonies, unless we restrict our sample to empires, kingdoms and the two leading republics: Netherlands and Venice. Then the colonial states come up to a mean of 4.2 orders per country, while the states without colonies stay at 3.3.

The great powers evidently dominated the system of orders as they dominated and formed the pattern for most other things in Europe. We expect this domination to apply also to the differentiation of the orders: states with more power should have more orders of all kinds than states with less power, and Catholic states should have more orders than non-catholic states. We test these hypotheses in the following table:

Proportion of states with high orders in one class, orders of military merit, of civil merit and orders for ladies, the states classified according to political power and religion.

Political power	Religion	Proportion of states with:			
		High orders	Military orders	Civil orders	Orders for ladies
Great	Catholic	3/3	2/3	2/3	2/3
	Non-catholic	3/4	2/4	2/4	1/4
	Sum	6/7	4/7	4/7	3/7
Middle range	Catholic	7/8	2/8	0/8	1/8
	Non-catholic	3/5	1/5	1/5	0/5
	Sum	10/13	3/13	1/13	1/13
Small	Catholic	5/16	3/16	1/16	1/16
	Non-catholic	7/26	2/26	0/26	0/26
	Sum	12/42	5/42	1/42	1/42

The states with more political power had orders in higher proportions in fourteen cases out of sixteen and the Catholic states had higher proportions in eleven cases out of twelve. We have, however, already tested the same hypothesis for the sum of orders, and thus we find only that the same general combination pattern of the powerful and the Catholic states held for all four types of orders.

We have studied only four factors influencing the state orders. We realize that a large number of other factors might be of just as much or more importance. Technically a study of the interaction between a large number of variables is not very difficult but exceedingly boring, and so we avoid this problem as long as possible and do not return to it until in the last chapter.

Chapter 6
The Orders During the French
Revolution and in
the Napoleonic States

We have tried to analyse the changing goals of the Knighthood
orders and then the functions they were able to perform for the
sovereigns of Europe. We have in the previous chapter demonstrated an association between the power of the states, or rather of
their sovereigns, and the number of orders they could use to create
status and reward merits. But if the sovereigns lost their status, what
happened to the orders?

France is the first country we study in detail from this point of
view. The general French opinion about orders is most easily studied
in the case of the Hospitallers in Malta, as there are two interesting
volumes on this subject: Roderick Cavaliero: *The Last of the Crusaders*, Hollis and Carter, London 1960 and Claire E. Engel: *Knights
of Malta*, Allen and Unwin, London 1963.

In 1786 the Grand Master of St. John of Jerusalem was Emanuel
de Rohan. When he got news of the elections in France for an
Estates-General, he wrote to the diplomatic representative of the
order in Paris, de Suffren, how the members of the order should
vote. Rohan wanted to keep the order out of French turmoil. He
wanted the members to preserve perfect detachment and behave
rather as members of a foreign, independent state than as "Frenchmen" (*The Last of the Crusaders*, p. 181).

The ambassador, de Suffren, was a famous hero and popular in
France. His death in 1789 was a blow to the order, and he was replaced by De Brillane, who had contacts with the Royal family and
started his office with a splendid feast in the Temple (once taken
over from the Templars) for his knights and a splendid sample of
the royal court.

Against the Grand Master's instructions, three of his knights had
been elected to the Estates-General. More strenuous was the fact

that de Brillane meddled in French internal policy. The National Assembly on the night of 4th—5th August abolished all feudal privileges, rights and dues. The king signed the decree, but de Brillane wrote him asking for its revocation or modification as far as the Hospitallers were concerned. The King passed the letter to the president of the National Assembly, who had it read on 30th November.

Armand-Gaston Camus, deputy for Paris, spoke in the Assembly about the letter: "To provide a reply to this statement, I demand that the establishments of the Order of Malta in France be suppressed." He made, however, no motion but wrote pamphlets against the order.

The Hospitallers still were of considerable use to the merchants in Marseille, Lyon, etc., for their trade with the Levant. To keep a French fleet to convoy the merchantmen, would cost far more than the revenues the order got from the French commanders. But of course the French opinion was against aristocrats, against officers reserved for nobility, against men wearing foreign decorations. Still, as long as the members of the order kept the French laws, as their Grand Master had bidden them, which they did, the Hospitallers could not be brought before the law—unless the law was changed.

The National Assembly decreed on the 11th August that titles owned by secular and religious bodies were to be abolished, but all *rentes foncières,* which were not of feudal origin, could be redeemed. The case of the Hospitallers was discussed with great gusto. Mirabeau, who was a bailiff of the order, defended it vigorously, pointing out, that if the French rents were stopped, the order would be too poor to keep Malta and would have to sell out, either to Great Britain or Russia. The Chambers of Commerce in Marseilles, Bordeaux and Lyon stressed the same point and the high value of Malta's protection of the Levantine trade. The king also sent a message to the National Assembly in favor of the Hospitallers, but the Assembly stuck to the original decree and the king had to sanction it on the 11th of August.

Grand Master de Rohan was willing to tell his knights to pay the new taxes, keep the new laws and avoid irritating the general opinions, but he was not willing to accept alterations in the constitution or indemnifications from royal domains or from the Church of France. "Our cause is that of the king of France inasmuch as we are inclined to resist the abolition of distinctions reserved to the nobility, and to perpetuate a military order whose utility is recognized and which has always deserved well of His Majesty. We profess a perfect devotion to the sacred person of Louis XVI and our determination never to separate our interest from those of the Crown." (Cavaliero: *The Last of the Crusaders*, p. 187.)

The knights of Malta thus made the king's cause theirs although they were subjects of an independent order. The members of the French Royal orders of course had the same attitudes toward king and country, only to a higher degree. They saw nobility as the main source of talents to be used by king and crown for high offices, they took their vows of loyalty to the sovereign and his house to the letter, they expected status and veneration from all the subjects in the country, also from judges and police. They represented the establishment and they expected it to be accepted simply because it traditionally had been accepted. But at the same time they were unable to defend it verbally against the new ideology and its slogan about liberty, equality and brotherhood.

Their ideology could not be defended and they lost one part of its official foundation after the other. The feudal privileges were already gone: on the 28th October the Assembly suspended all vows in religious houses, on 6th November all distinctions of rank were abolished and on November 28th all those who had been exempted from paying taxes were to pay it retrospectively.

The order of Malta still hoped that the Assembly would pay back at least some of the lost *rentes foncières*. On 29th July 1790 the order pointed out that its ships cruised off the Spanish east coast to protect French merchantmen from the Barbary pirates, and asked for a decision. Camus entered in the discussion: "The time has come for us to decide whether the Orders of the Holy Ghost, of St. Lazarus, of Mount Carmel and of Malta are to continue". (Cavaliero: *The Last of the Crusaders*, p. 190.)

King Louis XVI and his family tried to escape from Paris toward the end of June 1791. He was caught at Varennes and the reaction showed how little status now remained for the royalty. It was rumored that the Hospitallers had lent money to the king for the flight. On the 30th July, 1791 the Assembly decreed that a Frenchman belonging to an order of knighthood, founded on birth rights, would lose his citizenship in the country. On the 10th August, Danton lead a mob towards the Tuileries and the king fled to the Assembly. Four days later the royal family was served a supper in the Hotel of the

Grand Prior of France, who had left the country, and then placed in the tower of the Temple. The ambassador of the Hospitallers protested against this violation of the order's property, but the Assembly considered the order no longer to possess any.

The army raised by the emperor and commanded by the duke of Brunswick slowly made its way into France. The Assembly desperately tried to raise money for the defences and on the 19th September the Hospitallers' land and property was declared forfeited to the state.

When the danger from Brunswick's army was gone, King Louis was brought out of the Temple, tried and executed. Then the last part of the chivalry ideology was gone: the sacred person of the king had lost not only power to protect his knights and their status among his people but also had been accused, tried, sentenced and punished like a common man.

The New Ideology

We have no intention here to describe the very complicated ideologies bound up with the French Revolution. We are not experts in that field and looking only for a set of factors useful for the description of states and their changes when we analyse the orders of knighthood and their functions in Europe after the French Revolution.

We have to point out, however, that the slogan of the revolution: liberty, equality and brotherhood, had a tremendous effect, but not in the short run. The first French republic did not last long. Napoleon made himself first consul in 1799 and emperor in 1804. Then liberty in the original meaning was gone, if it ever had been there. Brotherhood had never been achieved, but equality still remained in the sense of equality before the law. Napoleon certainly did consider his own courtiers, his own marshals or the knights, officers, commanders of his own orders as raised far above common subjects, but they had no legal privileges.

The ideology of the revolution was accepted by many intellectuals in Germany, in Italy and in England, but its effect was quickly counteracted by the revolutionaries themselves. The beheading of King Louis created much ill will. Far more important was the personal contacts with the French soldiers, fighting the tyrants and their hired mercenaries, liberating the people from the extorsions of the bureaucrats, making all men equals and behaving like brothers to everyone. The French soldiers certainly did fight the tyrants and their hired armies, and they fought well, so well that few European countries escaped very personal contacts with them, but otherwise they were very far from the expectations of the peoples they liberated.

Why were the French armies so successfull? We have to take a look at the traditional armies of Europe at this time. They were hired. A high officer would be asked to raise a regiment. He would quickly use his contacts to collect a number of officers around him and some old soldiers, make them sergeants and send them round the country to recruit young men, attracted by the perfect uniform in clear colours, by the traditional glory of the soldier, by the silver coins shown by the sergeant, by the regular meals or by the chance to get away from creditors or even petty crimes. They did not realize in time, that the military glory was reserved for the officers, that soldiers who accepted the silver coins of the recruiting sergeant had little chance for promotion but to corporal or sergeant, that discipline was very hard, possibly owing to difficulty to handle the frustrated men and to the fighting technique of steady infantry lines firing salvoes at each other and reloading as machines to the orders of their officers, some twenty orders necessary for the operation. Wellington spoke of his British soldiers as "the scum of the earth". He meant it.

The soldiers' pay was small, but the colonel had many of them and it took a long time to train them in the exercise necessary to make them efficient marching lines on the battlefield, firing and reloading only at command and able to keep the exact distances necessary for changing the lines into squares when cavalry threatened to attack. The regiment thus represented, after all, a considerable economic investment and had to be handled carefully, especially in war, so that men were lost only by enemy action or by execution, not by bad food, dysenteria or desertion, lack of food or tents. The commissariat had to bake bread, buy food and in principle pay in cash for all services from the civil population. And the officers had to be careful so that equipment was available, shoes and cloaks provided, marches not to long, tents brought by horses and wagons.

The small, professional, German armies thus moved slowly and cautiously, with a large train, tents, regular pay and full rations, but also a full ration of bullying officers, despise and fear of responsibility. When they entered France they met a hardening resistance and the battle of Valmy, although undecided, forced them to give up their march for Paris. But the French mobilization produced armies of a new kind. Many men and youngsters joined their ranks for ideological reasons: to defend their country and their new ideals. The large number of willing recruits also could be given good and enthusiastic officers, as the well-trained non-commissioned officers from the old royal French army now could be promoted according to their ability. The French armies thus grew up at a high speed, larger than anybody could have expected, learning quickly how to fight. The lack of money made it impossible to equip them with canvas tents, wagons and horses. The French armies had to "live on the country" as their supplies could not be carried in convoys and they soon made an art of the necessity. They had little to hamper them and so they made quicker and longer marches than hired troops.

The modern European wars took form in 1792: the ruthless use of the nation's full strength, rapid movements, bivouacs, requisitions and this peculiar mixture of violence and elation, quick tempered bravery and perseverance against misfortunes, that would drive a hired army to wholesale desertion. The outcome of the clash between modern French armies and the professional armies was given.

The French ideas of Liberty, Equality and Fraternity had spread like fire in Central Europe, but when French armies followed the French ideas, their way of "living on the country", of requisition or just plundering, of pressing cities or villages for money etc., demonstrated forcibly the differences between ideology and behavior. The ideology certainly was there, but hungry men did not think of their ideals until they were satisfied. And officers probably were able to rationalize their personal greed with the help of some phrases from their original ideology.

The revolutionary ideology probably meant much at the birth of the French new model armies, but its value from the military point of view decreased quickly. And so some of the traditional values had to be reestablished. Already as First consul, Napoleon introduced his new order: the Legion of Honor, as an emperor he reintroduced nobility. The Legion of Honor was built on the pattern of St. Louis, had the same red ribbon but four classes and later five, as a Grand cross class, called Grand Eagle, was added. Napoleon in 1808 established the Palms, in two classes, for scholars and teachers, not quite up to the level necessary for the Legion of Honor. Northern Italy was made part of France, with Napoleon as king of Italy. His vice-king, Éugene de Beauharnais resided in Florence and handled the Order of the Iron Crown in three classes. And in 1811, Napoleon eventually created the Order of Reunion in three classes, to be used also for the new French subjects in the German, Italian, Dutch or Swiss countries incorporated with France.

Napoleon's victories made it possible to create around France a ring of kingdoms ruled by members of the house of Bonaparte: his brother Joseph first king of Naples, then in Spain, his brother Louis in Holland, his brother Jerome in Westphalia, his brother in law Joachim Murat in Naples, his step-son Eugene vice-king in Italy. All these Napoleonic states abolished the old orders, if any, and introduced new ones: Holland got the order of the Union and the order of Merit, both in 1806, Naples the order of the two Sicilies in 1808, Spain the Royal order in 1808 and Westphalia the Crown of Westphalia in 1809.

France hade incorporated the Western side of the Rhine. The small German states there disappeared, their princes receiving considerable sums for giving up their rights, unless they were princes of the Catholic church: ecclesiastical electors, bishops, etc. These lands the French just took over, if situated on their side of the Rhine, and if situated on the eastern side, it was used to compensate Baden, Bavaria, Württemburg etc. for their land lost on the western side. The Grand Master of the Hospitallers and the German Master of the Teutonic order thus lost their last domains in 1809.

Many of the remaining German states on the Rhine got far larger territories this way and Napoleon, always willing to distribute status instead of resources, raised the rank of the more important sovereigns: the electors of Bavaria and Saxony were made kings and so was the duke of Württemburg while Baden, Berg, Frankfort, Hesse-Darmstadt and Würzburg were raised to grand-duchies, a number of princedoms like Anhalt-Bernburg or Nassau promoted to duchies, etc. The Holy Roman Empire of the German Nation was made a nullity and dissolved by its emperor, Francis, in 1806. He remained emperor all the same, as Austria had been declared an empire in 1804. The German states but Prussia and Austria formed in 1806 the Rhine Confederation, allied with France and used as a base for the Napoleonic armies. The sovereigns in the confederation often created orders of military merit in several classes, meant for the troops they now had to raise. So there is an interesting alliance here between the military goal of the French revolution, still important, and the hard stress on loyalty of the subjects to Napoleon, his house and the surviving houses of his allies, learning little liberty, no brotherhood, but some equality before the law.

Orders of Knighthood in European States from 1792 to 1810

We are interested in the changing functions of the European orders of knighthood between 1792 and 1810. We need not describe the complicated history of this period, we need only use a restricted number of factors to describe the European states after 1792 from our very narrow field of interest. We have previously used four such factors or variables: the rank of the sovereign, the political power of the country, religion and colonies. We retain these four and add three more. These seven variables were, however, viewed very differently by traditional Europeans, by the revolutionaries and by the men loyal to the Napoleonic ideology. We thus have to discuss each factor from different viewpoints.

1. The rank of the sovereign traditionally was the measure of his competence, his status and his rights over his subjects. From the revolutionary point of view, the higher rank the sovereign possessed, the more power and the stronger army, the larger bureaucracy, the more incompetent administration, but still the better able to rob the subjects of their liberty, their equality and their fraternity. And then back to the compromises of the Napoleonic sympathisers: The higher rank, the better adjusted to French policy, the more willing to modernize law, commerce and army, the better able to obtain privileges out of the emperor.

How did this factor influence the European orders? Well, we first must realize that many states of the 62, we studied for the year 1792, now are gone and others have come; besides many have acquired higher rank and more land. So we have to start by defining our new sample of 56 states. Now we have four empires: Austria, France, Russia and Turkey, fourteen kingdoms: Bavaria, Denmark, Great Britain, Italy (although formally united with France), Naples, Netherlands (or Holland, later united with France), Portugal, Prussia, Sardinia (only the island itself left), Saxony, Sicily (formally Naples), Spain (two different kingdoms) and Sweden, the six grand duchies of Baden, Berg, Frankfort, Hesse-Darmstadt, Warsaw and

Würzburg and then thirty states of lower rank. We have then skipped some of the smallest members of the Rhine Confederation (none of them surviving the Vienna Congress).

The number of orders in the states is now of less interest than whether they have got orders at all, and what kind of orders. We present these data as percentages and compare only the higher ranking sovereigns down to grand dukes with those lower on the scale: dukes, princes, and heads of republics. See table 1.

More states on the higher rank level possessed orders in 1810 than in 1792, but fewer states on the lower level. This tendency was particularly strong for military orders and civil orders, which generally used the Napoleonic pattern of the Legion of Honor. High orders in one class and special orders for ladies were not used by Napoleon and so were more rare in 1810 than in 1792, as some of the states formerly possessing them had lost their sovereignity and few or no new orders of these kinds had been founded.

These data suggest that high ranking sovereigns were more anxious for orders in 1810 than in 1792, but also that some subtle pressure prevented the sovereigns lower in rank from creating orders of their own.

2. The political power of the countries we study in the same way as the rank of the sovereigns by dividing the states in two groups: nineteen states of strong or middle power, thirty-seven with little power. We compare the set of orders in these two classes of states in 1792 with their sets in 1810. Data given in table 2.

The general pattern is a lower percentage of states having orders in 1810 than in 1792, but the orders open for civilians, just as the French Legion of Honor, have clearly increased and so form an exception.

This is what we should expect, since the Legion of Honor could be used to reward the civilians, expecially in the more powerful states and on a grander scale in 1810 than in 1792. Why? Well, we might say that the political power of the state was important to the citizens as it gave them more protection against foreign aggression; it was useful to merchants involved in international trading and to shipping. But in 1810 few of the states with great or middlesized political power did possess any power, at least not power enough to protect their citizens against foreign, that is French, aggression, to give the merchants involved in international trading a fair chance during the French Continental system or shipping a chance against

Table 1. Percentages of states possessing orders of different kinds, states according to rank of head.

Rank of head of state	No. of states		% with orders		% with high orders		% with military orders		% with civil orders		% with ladies orders	
	1792	1810	1792	1810	1792	1810	1792	1810	1792	1810	1792	1810
Grand duke or above	20	26	75	85	75	59	35	40	25	58	20	15
Remaining states	42	30	33	3	26	3	12	0	2	0	2	0
Sum	62	56	47	41	44	26	19	18	10	27	8	7

Table 2. Percentages of states possessing orders of different kinds, states according to political power.

Political Power	No. of states		% with orders		% with high orders		% with military orders		% with civil orders		% with ladies orders	
	1792	1810	1792	1810	1792	1810	1792	1810	1792	1810	1792	1810
Great or middle	19	19	79	74	79	47	37	32	26	63	21	16
Small states	43	37	33	25	28	16	12	11	2	8	2	3
Sum	62	56	47	41	44	26	19	18	10	27	8	7

Table 3. Percentages of states possessing orders of different kinds, states according to size of population.

Population size	No. if states		% with orders		% with high orders		% with military orders		% with civil orders		% with ladies orders	
	1792	1810	1792	1810	1792	1810	1792	1810	1792	1810	1792	1810
Above a million	20	20	80	85	80	55	35	45	25	70	20	20
Below a million	42	36	31	17	26	11	12	3	2	3	2	0
Sum	62	56	47	41	44	26	19	18	10	27	8	7

Table 4. Percentages of states possessing orders of different kinds, states according to their possession of or share in a university, 1792 and 1810.

University	No. of states		% with orders		% with high orders		% with military orders		% with civil orders		% with ladies orders	
	1792	1810	1792	1810	1792	1810	1792	1810	1792	1810	1792	1810
Yes	30	29	63	69	63	41	40	34	13	41	17	14
No	32	27	30	9	25	11	0	0	7	11	0	0
Sum	62	56	47	41	44	26	19	18	10	27	8	7

Orders during the French Revolution . . .

the British navy slowly taking over all colonies worth the trouble, blockading all the important harbors, sending small cruisers everywhere to sweep up even the coastal shipping of the Napoleonic countries. Under these conditions the civilian certainly should need rewards of every kind.

3. The size of population is, for us, an important aspect of political power, but probably it was of far less importance in 1792. But as the small, professional armies were substituted by the large conscription armies, a large population meant a large reserve af Cannon fodder. We divide the states of 1810 in two groups: twenty with a million inhabitants or more; thirty-six with less than a million. The population data have generally been taken out of the Meyer's Konversations lexikon, 5 edition.

We study the population data in table 3.

We expect the countries with large populations to have more weight in 1810 than in 1792, when armies still were small and had to be hired. The data go in the direction we expected, larger differences between countries above and countries below the million in 1810 than in 1792. The tendency is, however, not very strong but in the cases of military orders and of orders similar to the Legion of Honor, both types used as rewards of military merits.

4. The universities are a good measure of the cultural level in a country. If the country has no university or does not share in one—as some of the small German states did—then its cultural level probably is low.

In 1792, 30 states had a university or shared the costs of one; in 1810 the number was 29. We expect at these times universities to be more common among the powerful, large states, which also possess orders and so universities should be associated with orders. We expect this tendency to be still more pronounced in 1810, than in 1792, as the costs of the war might force small states to close their university. See table 4.

The table shows that countries with universities used orders in a far higher proportion—as we expected—and this tendency seems to be stronger in 1810 than in 1792.

5. The religious factor is of interest in 1792, as the revolutionaries later abolished the religion for a while. Napoleon reestablished contacts with the Pope but held him under close control and incorporated Rome with the kingdom of Italy. The Catholic countries had, however, a stronger tradition of orders, but in 1810 the difference

Table 5. Percentages of states, possessing orders of different kinds, according to the religion of the states.

Religion	No. of states		% with orders		% with high orders		% with military orders		% with civil orders		% with ladies orders	
	1792	1810	1792	1810	1792	1810	1792	1810	1792	1810	1792	1810
Catholic	27	22	59	50	46	27	27	18	11	41	15	14
Non-catholic	35	34	37	35	43	26	14	18	9	18	3	3
Sum	62	56	47	41	44	26	19	18	10	27	8	7

Table 6. Percentages of states, possessing orders of different kinds, according to the states having colonies or not.

Colonies	No. of states		% with orders		% with high orders		% with military orders		% with civil orders		% with ladies orders	
	1792	1810	1792	1810	1792	1810	1792	1810	1792	1810	1792	1810
Colonies	7	7	86	100	86	57	43	29	14	71	14	14
No colonies	55	49	42	33	38	22	16	16	9	20	7	6
Sum	62	56	47	41	44	26	19	18	10	27	8	7

Orders during the French Revolution . . .

between them and the non-Catholic countries ought to be much reduced. Table 5 sums up the data.

Our expectation that the Catholic countries would have a stronger tendency to have orders in 1792 than in 1810 generally seems to be correct, but the trend is weak and in one case, the civil orders of the type Legion of Honor, goes decidedly in the opposite direction. We have, however, no easy explanation ready for this unexpected outcome.

6. Colonies were extremely important in 1810—if their products could be shipped to Europe. Sugar, coffee, cotton, spices, etc. were rare in Europe because of the British blockade. But if the colonial merchants suffered seriously, we expect that the governments tried to console them with other means, such as orders. And so we expect the colonial countries to have more orders than the countries without and we expect this difference to be larger in 1810 than in 1792, especially for the civil orders. See table 6.

The civil orders certainly have a larger difference in 1810 between states with and states without colonies than in 1792, but otherwise there are no great changes, only in the sum.

7. Loyalty to Napoleon could influence the number of orders, as the new Napoleonic states certainly would accept the revolutionary pattern of abolishing all former orders and then introduce a relative low number of new ones. Then the states opposed to Napoleon would be left with more orders and the new states with few or none. Our sample contains 15 states less loyal or even hostile: Andorra, Austria, Denmark, Great Britain, Monaco, Portugal, Prussia, Russia, San Marino, Sardinia, Sicily (Naples), Spain (Bourbon), Sweden, Switzerland (Helvetian republic), Turkey. The remaining 41 states we consider more loyal. Then these two types of states show the following differences:

Table 7. Percentages of states possessing orders of different kinds, according to the state's loyalty to Napoleon.

Attitude to Napoleon	No. of states	% with orders	% with high orders	% with military orders	% with civil orders	% with ladies orders
Hostile-Neutral	15	60	53	40	47	20
Loyal	41	34	17	10	20	3
Sum	56	41	26	18	27	7

The countries loyal to Napoleon have orders to a much less extent, which of course partly comes from the fact that they generally are much smaller. Still, our expectations certainly are fulfilled.

We could also have a look at the new orders created from 1792 to 1810, and then, of course, the countries with Napoleonic influence are of special interest. We divide our sample of 56 states from 1810 in five groups of states: 1) those with Napoleonic dynasties, 2) those under close control, 3) Austria, Denmark and Prussia, under remote control, 4) neutral Russia, Sweden and Turkey, and 5) hostile: Great Britain, Portugal, Sardinia, Sicily, and (Bourbon) Spain. Which of these countries created orders and what kind? See table 8.

The Napoleonic dynasties abolished all orders and so had to create new ones and they all used the pattern of the Legion of Honor, but in some cases added some more orders, such as the Palms in France. The Napoleonic allies in most cases were small states, but the larger of them did create new orders, generally of the same type as the Legion of Honor. Saxony and Württemberg, however, created high orders, Baden and Bavaria military orders.

Austria, Denmark, Prussia, etc., unwilling but still allies to France, should have less use for orders, but Austria, all the same, created the order of Leopold and a cross for field priests. The neutral states did not create any orders, but the states fighting for their lives against French armies certainly could use rewards and in some cases they were given the form of orders. King Ferdinand, protected on Sicily by Nelson's fleet, had created the order of St. Ferdinand in three classes and Portugal created the order of the Tower and the Sword with the same five classes as the Legion of Honor, but Portugal also instituted the order of Isabella for noble ladies.

We find thus that the position of the states in relation to Napoleonic France had a strong influence on their new orders.

8. The privileged nobility was a part of the social system attacked by the French revolutionaries, and the cry for equality was a challenge to it. Napoleon certainly created a new nobility, but he gave them titles, not privileges. The new French law, Code Napoleon, recognized no exceptions from the rule of equality before the law, and the countries receiving Napoleonic dynasties or reorganizing their new territories often followed the French pattern. We consider that in 1810 the privileges of the nobility were non-existent or drastically reduced in 16 countries, while they remained at least to a degree not to be ignored, in 40 countries.

Table 8. Table on the proportion of European states in 1810, creating new orders between 1792 and 1810.

Kind of new order	Napoleonic dynasties	Napoleonic allies	Andorra, Austria, Denmark, Monaco, Prussia, San Marino Switzerland	Russia, Sweden Turkey	Great Britain, Portugal, Sardinia, Sicily, Spain
High order, one class	0/6	2/35	0/7	0/3	0/5
Orders like Legion of Honor	6/6	5/35	1/7	0/3	2/5
Orders of military merit	1/6	2/35	1/7	0/3	2/5
Orders of civil merit	1/6	0/35	0/7	0/3	0/5
Orders for ladies	0/6	0/35	0/7	0/3	1/5

Table 9. Percentage of states, possessing orders of different kinds, according to privileges of the nobility.

Privileges of Nobility	No. of states		% with orders		% with high orders		% with military orders		% with civil orders		% with ladies orders	
	1792	1810	1792	1810	1792	1810	1792	1810	1792	1810	1792	1810
Privileges	55	40	53	33	49	33	22	20	11	10	9	8
No Privileges	7	16	0	69	0	13	0	13	0	19	0	6
Sum	62	56	47	41	44	26	19	18	10	27	8	7

We expect that the countries with a privileged nobility would often have the orders of the type reserved for nobility: the high orders, the military orders and the ladies' orders (but they would *not* have the orders similar to the Legion of Honor). These tendencies, however, should be weaker in 1810 than in 1792, when just a few countries like Switzerland, Andorra, San Marino, Frankfort lacked the privileged nobility. Table 9 sums up the data.

Actually the countries with a privileged nobility do have a higher proportion possessing high orders, military orders and ladies' orders than the countries without; these differences are also larger in 1792 than in 1810. The civil orders, however, show the opposite pattern as they were rare in 1792 and monopolized by the nobility states, but common in 1810 and especially in the Napoleonic countries lacking nobility with privileges.

The nobility pattern thus might have had some effect on the creation of orders, as the sovereigns had to cut these privileges down to reasonable size and then use high orders, etc. to console the nobility left with little power—that is, to use orders as rewards instead of nobility and nobility privileges.

We have then discussed seven variables characterizing the European states and have shown how they are associated with orders of different kinds. But these factors of course, interact also with one another. The small European states of 1810 generally were German principalities belonging to the Rhine Confederation, loyal to Napoleon, non-catholic, without colonies and most of them too small to have orders yet. This interaction changes rapidly in Europe and so we have better to go right through the history of the European orders and then sum up our data in interaction tables, one table for each year studied, to compare their end results.

Chapter 7
The Orders in 1819, after the Vienna Congress

The Napoleonic armies were at last beaten and Europe had to rebuild its productionsystem and try to handle the enormous debts the wars had brought with them. The governments and/or sovereigns thus had to reward the heroes of the Napoleonic wars and at the same time show their appreciation of the industrialists and civil servants helping the country to recover. They used, of course, orders as rewards. Several war-decorations or orders were created after 1810, as the French imperial armies were forced to retreat, Bourbon Spain, ruled by a junta, got the order of St. Ferdinand in 1811, Prussia the Iron cross in 1813, Austria the Artillery cross in 1814, Hesse-Cassel the order of the Iron Helmet in the same year, Sardinia the Savoyan order of Military Merit, the Netherlands the order of William, and Great Britain gave two new classes for officers to the order of the Bath, all three in 1815. The reestablished Bourbon kingdom of France reorganized most of the old orders, among them St. Louis for military merits, but also kept the Legion of Honor, exchanging the imperial crown on the badge for a royal one and the head of Napoleon for that of Henry IV.

The Legion of Honor was too popular to be abolished and its pattern of several classes, all of them open to officers as well as to representatives of civil service, science, arts, commerce and industry, still held a considerable attraction. Hannover created the order of the Guelf in 1815 along these lines, Saxe-Weimar added two new classes to the white Falcon in the same year and in 1816 Sardinia did the same with the order of St. Maurice and St. Lazarus.

We handle 56 states in our sample of 1819, and intend to describe the system of orders using factors similar to those we introduced in our description of 1810: rank of sovereigns, political power and diplomatic rank of the states, the size of their population, their religions, colonies, the political attitude of their dynasties and then their role in Metternich's political system: dominated by it or not.

Orders and the Rank of the Sovereign or Head of State

In 1819 three states can be given imperial rank: Austria, Russia and Turkey, sixteen royal rank: Bavaria, Denmark, France, Great Britain, Hannover, Netherlands, Norway, the Holy See, Poland, Portugal, Prussia, Saxony, Spain, Sweden and Württemberg, eight rank of Grand dukes: Baden, Hesse-Darmstadt, Luxemburg, Mecklenburg-Schwerin, Mecklenburg-Strelitz, Oldenburg, Saxe-Weimar and Toscana, one the rank of elector, Hesse-Cassel, and twenty-six had lower ranks. We thus divide our sample in twenty-six states with higher ranking sovereigns and twenty-six with lower ranking. We compare the proportions of states with the usual type of order among high and low ranking states and the states of 1819 with those of 1810. See table 1.

All differences between 1810 and 1819 are very small and re-stricted to the military orders, wich are a little more numerous in 1819. The higher ranking states differed may be a little less from the lower ranking states in 1819 than in 1810. Rank of states thus seems to mean practically the same in 1819 as in 1810 as far as the orders of knighthood are concerned.

Orders and the Political Power of the European Countries

We have not more than 18 countries in 1819, which can be considered as having some or great political power. We expect of course, these states to possess orders to a higher degree than the small states, but there is hardly a chance that this difference should be smaller in 1819 than in 1810. The data come this way in table 2.

Actually the difference between states with at least some political power and the small states was much larger in 1819 than in 1810, probably because some of the small ephemeral Napoleonic states used orders and were gone in 1819. There is now a very evident tendency among the influential states to use orders, while the smaller states have not yet taken over this pattern.

Table 1. Percentages of states possessing orders of different kinds, states according to rank of head, 1819.

Rank of head of state	No. of states		% with orders		% with high orders		% with military orders		% with civil orders		% with ladies orders	
	1810	1819	1810	1819	1810	1819	1810	1819	1810	1819	1810	1819
Elector or above	26	28	85	86	54	54	40	54	58	54	15	25
Remaining states	30	28	3	14	3	4	0	10	0	7	0	0
Sum	56	56	41	49	26	29	18	31	27	30	7	13

Table 2. Percentages of states possessing orders of different kinds, states according to political power, 1819.

Political Power	No. of states		% with orders		% with high orders		% with military orders		% with civil orders		% with ladies orders	
	1810	1819	1810	1819	1810	1819	1810	1819	1810	1819	1810	1819
Great or middle	19	18	74	83	47	77	32	72	63	77	16	39
Little or none	37	38	25	34	16	5	11	13	8	8	3	0
Sum	56	56	41	49	26	29	18	31	27	30	7	13

Orders and the Diplomatic Rank of the European Countries in 1819

Singer and Small have recently published an article: "The Composition and Status Ordering of the International System, 1815—1940" (World Politics XVIII, 1966, pp. 236—282) where they rank the states with diplomatic representations according to the number of states represented in the capital of the country, weighing each embassy or legation as to the rank of the representative in charge of it (ambassador 3 points, minister or envoy 2 points, chargé d'affaires 1 point) and to the number of states represented at his own capital. England is at the top of the list, Saxony, Baden, Württemberg, Hesse-Cassel, Hesse-Darmstadt and Portugal at the bottom.

Using this ranking list for 1820, we divide the European states in 22 states with diplomatic representation and 34 without. These two types of states should of course, differ considerably, not only because the diplomatic system uses orders of knighthood as a part of its career and contact pattern, but also because the important states use diplomacy as well as orders.

The difference between diplomatically represented states and the not represented is demonstrated in the following table:

Table 3. Percentages of states possessing orders of different kinds, states according to diplomatic rank. 1819.

Diplomatic rank	No. of states	% with orders	% with high orders	% with military orders	% with civil orders	% with ladies orders
Represented	22	87	68	73	73	32
Not represented	34	24	3	6	3	0
Sum	56	49	29	31	30	13

The diplomatic factor evidently is strongly associated with the system of knighthood orders.

Orders and the Size of Population

In 1819, two more states had passed the million and so we now have 22. Theoretically, we see no reason to expect much change since 1810

Table 4. Percentages of states possessing orders of different kinds, states according to size of population, 1819.

Size of Population	No. of states		% with orders		% with high orders		% with military orders		% with civil orders		% with ladies orders	
	1810	1819	1810	1819	1810	1819	1810	1819	1810	1819	1810	1819
Above one million	20	22	85	87	55	68	45	68	70	68	20	32
Below one million	36	34	17	24	11	3	3	9	3	6	0	0
Sum	56	56	41	49	44	29	18	31	27	30	7	13

Table 5. Percentages of states possessing orders of different kinds, states according to their possession or share in a university, 1819.

University	No. of states		% with orders		% with high orders		% with military orders		% with civil orders		% with ladies orders	
	1810	1819	1810	1819	1810	1819	1810	1819	1810	1819	1810	1819
Yes	29	28	69	75	41	46	34	57	41	54	14	22
No	27	28	9	23	11	11	0	7	11	7	0	3
Sum	56	56	41	49	26	29	18	31	27	30	7	13

on the relation between population and orders; but of course other variables can influence the relations. See table 4.

The size of the population is still a very important factor and possibly still more important in 1819 than in 1810. This could, however, be easily explained afterwards as the size of population must have rather strong associations with the political power as well as with the diplomatic rank of the states, both of them very important from our point of view.

Orders and Universities

We expect that the economic crisis in Europe after the Napoleonic wars prevented an expansion of the university system and so the important states tended to possess universities as well as orders, the unimportant states to have neither. We expect the association between orders and universities to be still stronger in 1819 than in 1810.

The states with universities thus tended to use orders to a higher degree than the states lacking universities or a share in them, as for instance the small dukedoms Saxe-Altenburg, Saxe-Goburg-Gotha, Saxe-Coburg-Saalfeld and Saxe-Meiningen had in the university of Jena, situated in Saxe-Weimar. The difference between states with universities and states lacking them seems to be more pronounced in 1819 than in 1810. See table 5.

Orders and the Religious Factor

The Catholic countries still had a number of medieval chivalry orders, but here we are interested not in the number of orders but in the system of orders. Did the countries possess orders of different kinds or not? Then the non-catholic countries by this time should have been able to catch up with the catholic countries rather well.

The Catholic countries had high orders, military orders and ladies' orders to a larger extent than the non-catholic countries, but otherwise the non-catholic countries seem to use some system of orders nearly as often as the Catholic countries. Table 6.

Orders and the Colonies

Colonies certainly could be more efficiently used in peacetime thus rewards to the colonial administration etc. should be more important

Table 6. Percentages of states possessing orders of different kinds, states according to official religion 1819.

Religion	No. of states		% with orders		% with high orders		% with military orders		% with civil orders		% with ladies orders	
	1810	1819	1810	1819	1810	1819	1810	1819	1810	1819	1810	1819
Catholic	22	20	50	55	27	45	18	40	41	40	14	25
Non-Catholic	34	36	35	44	26	19	18	28	18	25	3	6
Sum	56	56	41	49	26	29	18	31	27	30	7	13

Table 7. Percentages of states possessing orders of different kinds, states according to their colonies, 1819.

Colonies	No. of states		% with orders		% with high orders		% with military orders		% with civil orders		% with ladies orders	
	1810	1819	1810	1819	1810	1819	1810	1819	1810	1819	1810	1819
Yes	7	7	100	100	57	86	29	86	71	100	14	43
No	49	49	33	41	22	20	16	24	20	20	6	8
Sum	56	56	41	49	26	29	18	31	27	30	7	13

after the war. We expect a stronger association between colonies in 1819 than in 1810. See table 7.

The colonial powers thus possess high orders, military orders, civil orders and ladies' orders to a much larger extent than the countries without colonies and this tendency is far more pronounced in 1819 than in 1810.

Dynasties, Once Loyal to Napoleon, and their Orders

The Napoleonic dynasties were all gone in 1819, but there remained many dynasties in Germany: Baden, Bavaria, Saxony, Württemberg, etc.) which once had been given higher rank by Napoleon and remained loyal with him also after his defeat in Russia—for some time. These dynasties had often accepted the Napoleonic types of orders, and so we expect them to show a pattern different from the remaining countries in 1819. We can look at table 8.

Actually, the dynasties once loyal with Napoleon changed their system of orders very little if we compare them with the states loyal in 1810. We have, however, to keep in mind that in 1819 France, Spain, Netherlands, the two Sicilies and the former Westphalia had dynasties hostile toward Napoleon and so the loyal states now consisted mostly of small German states, once belonging to the Confederation of the Rhine.

States, Loyal to Metternich's European Policy

The Austrian Prime minister Metternich had a strong influence on the conference in Vienna and was able to organize a systematic interaction between the great European powers in order to guarantee the Territorial Status Quo (as the territories had been defined in Vienna) and also guarantee the reigning European dynasties their "legitimate sovereignty", which seemed to mean their autocracy. Austria, Russia and Prussia backed this policy and nearly all German and Italian small states followed Metternich's intentions. Great Britain, however, soon broke with Metternich and other countries, fourteen all together, followed. They were: Andorra, Denmark, France, Great Britain, Hannover, Luxemburg, Netherlands, Norway, Portugal, Sardinia, Saxe-Weimar, Spain, Sweden and Switzerland. The remaining 42 states we consider loyal or at least more loyal with Metternich. The many small loyal states thus felt secure

Table 8. Percentages of states possessing orders of different kinds, states according to the former attitude of their dynasties toward Napoleon, 1819.

Attitude to Napoleon	No. of states		% with orders		% with high orders		% with military orders		% with civil orders		% with ladies orders	
	1810	1819	1810	1819	1810	1819	1810	1819	1810	1819	1810	1819
Hostile—Neutral	15	23	60	65	53	48	40	56	47	52	20	26
Loyal	41	33	34	36	17	15	10	15	20	15	3	3
Sum	56	56	41	49	26	29	18	31	27	30	7	13

against aggression from abroad and just as secure in relation to the political opposition within the countries, working for liberal constitutions. There should be less orders needed in the countries loyal to Metternich, as there was little use of rewards in these states seeking stability not from citizens but from the secret police and the armies of Austria, Prussia and Russia.

Table 9. Percentages of states possessing orders of different kinds, states according to their loyalty to Metternich's policy, 1819.

Loyalty with Metternich	No. of states	% with orders	% with high orders	% with military orders	% with civil orders	% with ladies orders
Yes	42	45	24	29	22	10
No	14	57	43	43	57	27
Sum	56	49	29	31	30	13

There is a decidedly stronger tendency towards orders in states not loyal to Metternich's policy. This, of course, partly comes from the fact that nearly all the small German and Italian states followed Metternich and many of them were so small that they not yet had acquired orders.

Orders and Privileged Nobility

The privileges of the nobility at this time were shaken but still there in most of the European states. Some states such as Norway had practically no nobility left, some never had had one, San Marino for instance, and some, such as Bavaria, had followed the lead of the French revolutionaries and abolished all privileges of nobility. France actually did not reestablish the noble privileges. In 1814, there was created a Chamber of peers, where the princes of the blood royal took seat together with a large number of peers, but these were nominated by the king and most of them came from the Napoleonic nobility, not from the émigrés.

All together 15 states in our opinion can be considered to have little or nothing left of nobility privileges. But these states would not be Napoleonic and so they might show other patterns. See table 10.

Actually there is a shift so that the states with no nobility privileges

Table 10. Percentages of states, possessing orders of different kinds, according to privileges of the nobility, 1819.

Privileges of nobility	No. of states		% with orders		% with high orders		% with military orders		% with civil orders		% with ladies orders	
	1810	1819	1810	1819	1810	1819	1810	1819	1810	1819	1810	1819
Yes	40	41	33	61	33	37	20	39	10	34	8	17
No	16	15	69	13	73	7	13	13	69	13	6	0
Sum	56	56	41	49	26	29	18	31	27	30	7	13

in 1810 had a strong tendency to use orders and especially orders similar to the Legion of Honor, but in 1819 the Napoleonic states among them had reestablished the privileges (but France) and the new set of states, such as Norway, neither had privileges nor orders. This means that nobility privileges and orders are associated in 1819. They were not in 1810. But in 1819 and from then on, nobility privileges no longer were obstacles for the sovereigns but, on the contrary, part of the establishment surrounding them.

Chapter 8
The New European Orders and Their Spacing in Time

We have decided from the start, that times of stress, such as wars and revolutions, might be interesting for us, as we expect hard pressed governments and/or sovereigns to use orders as rewards to larger extent when rewards are badly needed by fighting armies, ambitious civil servants, efficient industrialists, etc., helping to mobilize all resources of the country for one purpose or another. Still, this general idea does give us the two revolutions of 1830 and 1848 to study, but after those years the wars follow one another. So we had better take a general view, using first the revolutions and their reconstruction periods, then the wars to get the general picture of how many new orders and what kind of orders were created in Europe. We have divided the orders in 10 different kinds, among them the orders of Red Cross coming in use after the Geneva convention of 1864, and the special orders for courtiers. A late type are the orders created by the various orthodox churches. The table is given in the next page.

High orders are evidently both esteemed and rare, as the sovereigns had to make them very exclusive in order to keep them valuable. Most European states in the long run received an order of this type. Something similar can be said about the top military orders, reserved for the most prominent heroes of the right kind. The orders of the Red Cross are few and for very obvious reason created during or after wars. The orders open to civilians—most of them organized like the Legion of Honor—are the most common orders, making up nearly half of the new set. The orders for noble ladies are few, so are the orders of churches or the independent orders of St. John, organized for instance in England, Netherlands, etc. The orders for courtiers, to reward personal services to the sovereign or his house, are very few, but so different in purpose from usual orders, that they still should be registered for themselves. The orders of Arts and Sciences are few in the start

Table 1. New orders created in Europe 1773—1914.

Kind of Orders	Period					
	1772—1791	1792—1812	1813—1819	1820—1829	1830—1832	183.—1847
1. High orders in one class	2	2	2		3	1
2. Military orders		5	7		1	1
3. Orders of the Red Cross						
4. Orders open to civilians	1	17	14	2	10	15
5. Orders for ladies	1	2	2	1		
6. Orders of churches, of St. John		3				
7. Orders of Royal courts						
8. Orders of Art and Science			1		1	
9. Orders of Colonial administration						4
10. Orders of Industry and Agriculture	1	1				
11. Sum of Orders	5	30	26	3	15	21
Number of States, Approx.	68	67	56	56	57	57
Mean new orders per year and 50 states	0.2	2.0	3.4	0.3	4.4	1.2

but slowly become more popular toward the end of the nineteenth century. The orders for soldiers or civil servants in the colonial administrations are used especially by the French government; creating fifteen of them between 1837 and 1913. Then eventually some orders of Industry and Agriculture are created toward the end of the nineteenth century.

The spacing of the orders in time is of more interest. Before 1792 new orders were created very sparingly. Then suddenly orders are created to a large extent between 1792 and 1812, still more lavishly in the last years of the Napoleonic wars and the years next to them when the heroic deeds had to be rewarded and the diplomatic and/or economic efforts of the peace appreciated. But after 1819 Metternich's Holy Alliance actually succeeded to control at least the creation of new orders. Only three were needed in 1820 —1829. But then we have a new revolution, not because too few orders had been created, but possibly because there had been too few rewards for initiative and innovations, too much repression of critique and liberal constitutional ideas. The years 1830—1832

1848–1852	1853–1856	1857–1865	1866–1872	1873–1884	1885–1894	1895–1904	1905–1914	Sum
1		2	1	2	1	4	3	24
2	2	2	2	3	3	2		30
		1	2	2	1		2	8
7	4	11	6	6	2	1	5	101
	1		1	2	1		2	13
				1	2	1	1	8
		1				1	1	3
	1			1	2	2	1	9
		5		2	6	4	4	25
				1	1	1	1	6
10	8	22	12	20	19	16	20	227
59	59	59	45	46	46	46	48	
1.7	1.7	2.0	1.9	1.8	2.1	1.7	2.1	

certainly saw a large number of new orders; some of them in the new countries or new dynasties as France, Belgium or Greece, but still more created by dynasties scared by rebellions and anxious to create feelings of love and respect—as if that could be done by distributing badges of new orders designed with symbols such as the "love knot" (symbolizing the love of a grateful people).

The period between 1833 and 1847 saw a number of orders created, but we can consider it a peaceful time from our point of view as rather few new orders were created. Then there is a new revolutionary period, starting already in 1847 but culminating in 1848. This second set of revolutions was serious; in our opinion far more serious then the revolutions in 1830, and we expect it to result in a new set of orders. The number of orders created 1848—1852 is a little higher, yes, but not much higher. Why?

Well, we have looked upon the orders as means to compensate the citizens when they risk or give life, sweat and tears—or still worse, money—for their sovereign and their country. Citizens who resent this and prefer the risks of rebellion, may succeed, secure a new dynasty better adapted to their taste, and then expect to be rewarded not only with influence but also with orders. But if the original dynasty is able to weather the storm, their faithful followers need rewards whether the constitution had to be sacrificed or not. Should the subjects keep quiet in times of turmoil that is also a reason to reward them, although on a reduced scale.

So far we have discussed the problem from the sovereign's or the government's point of view. But the European peoples probably slowly realized the difference between the sovereign as a tyrant personally enjoying and misusing his power and the sovereign as the top manager of the establishment and the constitution. They realized that the sovereign actually was less important than the establishment and the constitution—or lack of constitution—forming the basis of the power structure. And then the sovereigns in the next step of the process learned to distinguish between rebellions directed towards them and their house, seen as intruders protected by bayonettes, and rebellions directed against the constitution.

The orders still belonged to the dynasty and so attacks on the dynasty, once beaten off, should be followed by new orders. If the sovereign had to reward his subjects with a new constitution he had less reason to use orders as rewards, still less reason to use them if no serious attempts were made upon the government and no reasons at all if he had to accept a new constitution but was able to get rid of it after a short time. We test this idea and divide our 57 states of 1830 in the following five categories:

New orders created in 1830—1847 in five categories of European states.

Categories of states	States creating	
	New orders	No new orders
1. States where the revolutionaries have acquired a new dynasty.	3	0
2. States with unsuccessful rebellion against dynasty.	2	1
3. States where constitution was attacked and permanently changed.	1	1
4. States without serious disturbances.	18	27
5. States given new constitutions, quickly withdrawn.	0	4

1. Revolution about 1830 and a new dynasty: Belgium, France, Greece.
2. Unsuccessful rebellion against dynasty: the Holy See, Luxemburg, Modena.
3. Attacks against the constitution, which is permanently changed: Brunswick, Hannover.
4. States with no serious disturbances: 45.
5. States given new constitution, which is quickly changed back: Baden, Hesse-Cassel, Saxony, Schwarzburg-Sondershausen.

We expect many orders during the time 1830—1847 in category 1, and then a decreasing tendency in the following categories until there should be no orders at all in the last category. See table p. 102.

There is actually a strong tendency in the direction we expected. New dynasties have to be generous with orders, and those who weathered the storms were rather generous too. If the constitution was changed, generosity was less necessary, still less if nothing happened and none if the sovereign first was forced to give a liberal constitution but then got control of the situation and felt strong enough to withdraw his promises.

But our real trouble was not the revolutions of 1830, but those of 1848. Is our model, that is our five categories, of any use for the period 1848—1856? Let us try:

New orders created in 1848—1856 in five categories of European states.

Categories	States creating	
	New orders	No new orders
1. State where the revolution was victorious (France).	1	0
2. Unsuccesful rebellions (in Austria-Hungary and 5 Italian states).	4	2
3. States with new permanent constitution (as Saxony).	3	8
4. States without serious disturbances.	5	16
5. States given new constitutions, quickly withdrawn.	0	14

These data still suit our model. And then we can explain the many orders after 1830 and the few after 1848 with the different reactions. The first period has three new dynasties, creating new orders, and only four dynasties first giving liberal constitutions, then withdrawing them and certainly not needing new orders. The second period of revolutions and their aftermath saw only one new state getting rid of the sovereign (France), but fourteen states given quickly withdrawn liberal constitutions and not in need of orders, as the sovereign hardly was or had been in danger, only the constitution. And so our model might explain at least a part of difference in pattern between the effects of the July revolution of 1830 and the February revolution in 1848.

A modern reader probably has just as much difficulty as we ourselves to take the orders and their roles in this interaction seriously. Well, we might try to show the importance attached to them in for instance the picture Stendahl draws of Italian policy in the beginning of the 19th century in *La Chartreuse de Parme*. Still better we could use the verses of Heinrich Heine, sharp critic of German culture and a very well versed sociologist using a delightful soft data approach. Der Kaiser von China (out of *Zeitgedichte*, 1839—46) describes the sovereign's classical conflict, when struggling to win power and popularity at the same time. We select two verses of his wishful thinking:

Die grosse Pagode, Symbol und Hort
Des Glaubens ist fertig geworden.
Die letzten Juden taufen sich dort
Und kriegen den Drachen Orden
Es schwindet der Geist der Revolution
Und es rufen die edelsten Mandschu:
"Wir wollen keine Konstitution,
Wir wollen den Stock, den Kantschu!"

Religion's symbol and safe retreat.
The great Pagoda, is now complete;
The last of the Jews are sprinkled
with water
And then receive the Dragon's Order.
Gone is the spirit of revolution!
"We don't want a constitution;
We are satisfied with the stick, the kantshu!
— Cry the noblest of the Manchu."
(Translated by Aaron Kramer)

And the citizens? The behavior pattern of the faithful Germans— deviating very much from the aggressive love of liberty displayed by old romans and new italians-Heine analyzed in *Zur Beruhigung*. We cite:

Wir sind Germanen gemütlich und brav,

We are Germans: kindly souls. Our sleep

Wir schlafen gesunden Pflanzen-
schlaf
Und wenn wir erwachen pflegt uns
zu dürsten,
Doch nicht nach dem Blute unserer
Fürsten.
Und wenn auch ein Brutus unter
uns wär.
Den Caesar fänd er nimmermehr
Vergeblich würd er den Caesar
suchen
Wir haben gute Pfefferkuchen.
Wir haben sechs und dreissig Herrn,
(Ist nicht zu viel!) und einen Stern
Trägt jeder schützend auf seinem
Herzen
Und er braucht nicht zu fürchten
die Iden des Märzen
Wir nennen sie Vater, und Vater-
land
Nennen wir dasjenige Land
Das erbeigentümlich gehört den
Fürsten
Wir lieben auch Sauerkraut mit
Würsten.

Is like the flowers'—wholesome and
deep—
And when we awake, our throats
are dry—
But it's not for princes' blood we
cry.
And should such a Brutus among us
rise.
He'd find no Ceasar-he'd strain his
eyes
In vain for Caesar everywhere;
The gingerbread we bake is rare.
We have six and thirty overseers
(That's not too many!) and each
one wears
A star on his heart, to keep him
from harm,
He can face the Ides without alarm.
We call them Fathers, and Father-
land
Is the name we place upon that
land
Which princes rule with inherited
right;
And sausage with sauerkraut's our
delight.

(Translated by Aaron Kramer)

The General Pattern of the Orders after the Revolution

After 1852, the number of new orders no longer varies very much. The European scene saw one war after another, saw new states emerging in the Balkan and saw approximately the same number of new orders all the time. But this does not say that the pattern of the orders changed only with the creation of new orders. Actually orders in many cases also disappear. Hannover, Hesse-Cassel and Nassau, all of them were incorporated with Prussia in 1866, as they sided up with Austria in the war of 1866. Then most of their orders also disappeared. Revolutions, of course, also affect the set of orders, as the old set generally is substituted for a new one, unless some are so popular that it is easier to reorganize them and change the insignia: the imperial crown might replace the laurel wreath of the republic, the mural crown replace the royal, the heads of sovereigns in the medallions replace or are replaced by heads of classic gods, etc. But this means that there is much more change in the European set of orders than our table can tell us about. We still have to choose some definite years to inventory the orders. We have chosen the years of 1832, 1872, 1914, 1925, and 1946. And so we start to describe the orders in 1832 and 1872 with the same technique as we already have used for 1792, 1810 and 1819.

Orders and the Rank of the Sovereign in 1832 and 1872

We have 57 states in 1832, but in 1872 a number of small states in Italy and Germany had been incorporated by larger states and only 45 remained. We still define high rank in 1832 as Elector or above, but in 1872 as Grand Duke or above, as Hesse-Cassel, the only state ruled by an elector, had been incorporated by Prussia. We expect that, as the pattern of orders is more and more accepted, also by small states, the high ranking states will more often have orders than the low ranking, but this difference should be smaller in 1872 than in 1832. Table 2 gives the data.

Orders actually were more common in 1872 than in 1832, and the states with low rank now came rather near to the high ranking as far as the orders open to civilians are concerned (type the Legion of Honor), but they are still lacking high orders, military orders and orders for noble ladies.

Orders and the Political Power of the States in 1832 and 1872

In 1832, 20 states could be considered to have great or some power, while 37 had no or little power. In 1872, the number of states with much or some power has been reduced to 15 and so 30 remain with none or little power. We present our data in the following table. We expect states with some political power to have more orders, but the states with none or little power should come nearer to the powerful pattern in 1872 than in 1832. See table 3.

There are more orders in 1872 than in 1832 and the states with little political power have come rather close to the pattern of the powers as only three of them (Andorra, Liechtenstein and Rumania)

Table 2. Percentages of states possessing orders of different kinds, according to the rank of the sovereign or head of state, 1832 and 1872.

Rank of head of state	No. of states		% with orders		% with high orders		% with military orders		% with civil orders		% with ladies orders	
	1832	1872	1832	1872	1832	1872	1832	1872	1832	1872	1832	1872
Elector of above	29	25	83	100	59	64	55	52	80	100	24	28
Remaining states	28	20	7	80	0	5	4	10	4	80	0	0
Sum	57	45	46	91	30	38	30	33	42	91	12	16

Table 3. Percentages of states possessing orders of different kinds, states according to the political power of the states, 1832 and 1872

Political Power	No. of states		% with orders		% with high orders		% with military orders		% with civil orders		% with ladies orders	
	1832	1872	1832	1872	1832	1872	1832	1872	1832	1872	1832	1872
Great or middle	20	15	95	93	75	67	65	67	85	93	35	33
Little or none	37	30	19	90	5	23	11	17	19	90	0	0
Sum	57	45	46	91	30	38	30	33	42	91	12	16

lacked orders in 1872 (just as Switzerland among the states with some political power). But the less influential states evidently used just one type of order, the one open also to civilians and in several classes.

Orders and the Diplomatic Rank of the European Countries in 1832 and 1872

Singer and Small's tables give the following rank to the European states in 1832: England, France, Russia, Austria, Turkey, Netherlands, Prussia, The Two Sicilies, Denmark, the Holy See, Spain, Sweden, Bavaria, Sardinia, Saxony, Switzerland, Tuscany, Württemberg, Baden, Hesse-Cassel, Greece, Hesse-Darmstadt, Portugal, Belgium and 33 states lacking representation. They give for 1874: France, England, Germany, Austria, Russia, Turkey, Italy, Belgium, Spain, Portugal, Netherlands, Sweden, Denmark, Switzerland, Greece, 30 states thus with no representation of their own abroad.

We expect that the countries with diplomatic representation will have orders in a higher proportion than the states without and that this tendency will be less pronounced in 1872 than in 1832. Our data are presented in table 4.

Differences between diplomatically active states and non-active states are much larger in 1832 than in 1872 and as usual very small for the civil orders.

Orders and the Size of Population

In 1832, 24 states had more than one million inhabitants and 33 had less. In 1872, 23 states had more than a million, 22 had less. We expect the more populous states to have more orders but we expect that when it comes to orders open to civilians the less populated states will be rather near. Our data are presented in table 5.

The less populous states actually had the same proportion of states with orders open to civilians as the more populous states in 1872, but far lower proportions for the other kinds of orders.

Orders and the Universities

In 1832 a little more than half the number of European countries possessed or had a share in universities, in 1872 the proportion had risen to 60 %. The universities in Germany were important as the

Diplomatic representation	No. of states 1832	1872	% with orders 1832	1872	% with high orders 1832	1872	% with military orders 1832	1872	% with civil orders 1832	1872	% with ladies orders 1832	1872
Yes	24	15	96	93	64	67	63	60	88	93	28	47
No	33	30	9	90	6	23	6	20	9	90	0	0
Sum	57	45	46	91	30	38	30	33	42	91	12	16

Table 5. Percentages of states possessing orders of different kinds, states according to their size of population in 1832 and 1872.

Population	No. of states 1832	1872	% with orders 1832	1872	% with high orders 1832	1872	% with military orders 1832	1872	% with civil orders 1832	1872	% with ladies orders 1832	1872
Above 1 million	24	23	92	91	71	61	64	61	88	91	28	31
Below 1 million	33	22	12	91	0	14	6	5	9	91	0	0
Sum	57	45	46	91	30	38	30	33	42	91	12	16

The New European Orders and Their Spacing in Time

only places where some—although closely watched—political discussion could take place during the time of the Holy Alliance and the universities on the whole tolerated far more liberal opposition than any other sector of the states. Universities thus could be expected to oppose not only autocratic governments but also their rewards and orders. On the other hand, there was a strong tendency to respect and reward learning and science, to accept the professors as civil servants, to give them rank and recognition. Orders reserved for arts and science are created. But these effects we probably will be unable to detect in our data. There we should rather expect the powerful, populous states to have universities as well as orders and this tendency ought to be more pronounced in 1872 than in 1832. See table 6.

We get the results we expected as universities still tend to be dependent of the resources of the countries.

Orders and the Dominant Religion of the State

We found earlier that the Catholic countries paid more attention to orders, partly because some medieval orders survived in them, partly because the majority of the small states without orders were German protestant principalities. A number of these disappeared before 1872, but so did most of the small Italian principalities. Then we anticipate that the difference between catholic and non-catholic countries will decrease a little between 1832 and 1872. See table 7.

Actually, the Catholic countries used orders to a higher extent in 1832, but in 1872, the non-catholic countries clearly surpass them, although not in high orders, military orders or ladies' orders.

Orders and Colonies

The same seven colonial powers—with Denmark and Sweden at the end of the list—still differ clearly from the other countries, but during this time the French colonial administration started to support the native princes in their protectorates in their endeavors to create orders of their own, actually used mostly to reward the high representatives of the French government. These colonial orders in our opinion thus should be considered here as European, as the majority of the rewarded were European and these orders probably made it eaiser to recruit administrators and officers for service in otherwise

Table 6. Percentages of states possessing orders of different kinds, states according to their possession or share in universities, 1832 and 1872.

Universities	No. of states		% with orders		% with high orders		% with military orders		% with civil orders		% with ladies orders	
	1832	1872	1832	1872	1832	1872	1832	1872	1832	1872	1832	1872
Yes	29	27	76	92	45	48	52	52	72	92	24	26
No	28	18	14	88	14	22	7	6	11	88	0	0
Sum	57	45	46	91	30	38	30	33	42	91	12	16

Table 7. Percentages of states possessing orders of different kinds, states according to their dominant religion, 1832 and 1872.

Dominant Religion	No. of states		% with orders		% with high orders		% with military orders		% with civil orders		% with ladies orders	
	1832	1872	1832	1872	1832	1872	1832	1872	1832	1872	1832	1872
Catholic	20	13	55	85	40	54	40	46	50	87	25	31
Non-catholic	37	32	41	93	24	31	24	28	38	93	5	9
Sum	57	45	46	91	30	38	30	33	42	91	12	16

little attractive colonies. But this will not influence the order system in general. Our data are presented in table 8.

There are large differences between the colonial powers and the remaining states, as the colonial powers use orders to a high degree, but the differences are very much the same in 1832 as in 1872.

Urbanization and Orders

Different countries define towns and rural areas differently and there are no simple statistics available. We are, however, more afraid of losing information that might be of interest than of introducing unreliable variables and so we shall try to estimate the degree of urbanization in the European countries using statistics from the official sources, from *Meyer's Konversations lexikon* and from Adna Ferrin Weber: *The Growth of Cities in the Nineteenth Century*. Cornell University Press. New York 1965, 2nd ed.

Weber defines urban population as the percent living in cities with more than 10,000 inhabitants and gives percentages for a number of states in 1800, in 1850 and 1890. Here, we actually are not interested in urbanization in itself, we rather use urbanization as a measure of industrialization, as industrialization is associated with organization of the workers and democratization. We cannot use Weber's population at all, as soon as they lack a city above 10,000. We have instead to accept for instance many of the small German principalities as urbanized although the cities often did not reach up to the critical number of 10,000. Data in table 9.

The more urbanized states generally had more orders of all kinds, but this tendency may be less pronounced in 1872 than in 1832.

For the year 1872, we also study the variable density of population, but we shall not present the data here.

Table 8. Percentages of states possessing orders of different kinds, states according to their possession of colonies or not, in 1832 and 1872.

Colonies	No. of states		% with orders		% with high orders		% with military orders		% with civil orders		% with ladies orders	
	1832	1872	1832	1872	1832	1872	1832	1872	1832	1872	1832	1872
Yes	7	7	100	100	86	71	86	86	100	100	47	29
No	50	38	39	90	22	32	22	29	34	90	8	13
Sum	57	45	46	91	30	38	30	33	42	91	12	16

Table 9. Percentages of states possessing orders of different kinds, states according to their estimated urbanization, in 1832 and 1872.

Urbanization	No. of states		% with orders		% with high orders		% with military orders		% with civil orders		% with ladies orders	
	1832	1872	1832	1872	1832	1872	1832	1872	1832	1872	1832	1872
More urbanization	18	17	77	100	44	35	50	53	77	100	11	18
Less urbanization	39	28	31	86	23	40	21	21	26	86	12	14
Sum	57	45	46	91	30	38	30	33	42	91	12	16

Chapter 9
The European Orders before and during World War I

At this time all European monarchies but Liechtenstein had built up sets of orders corresponding to or surpassing their ambitions to reward useful citizens. But many of the small monarchies were parts of the imperial Germany and thus had no diplomatic representation of their own and no political power abroad. The Catholic states still had a lead in the expansion of orders, as they nominally kept several of the medieval orders. This is shown in the following table:

Mean number of chivalry orders in European states of 1914, states according to power and religion.

Religion	Great powers (7)	States of the middle range (14)	Small states (27)
Catholic	14.3	12.3	5.4
Non-catholic	11.8	3.8	2.3

The rank of the sovereign still is important:

Number of orders in the European states of 1914, before World War I, according to the rank of the sovereign:

Empires (with the British Empire and Turkey)	Mean of 12.8 orders
Kingdoms (15) and the Holy See	6.8 orders
Grand duchies (7)	2.9 orders
Duchies and princedoms	1.4 orders
Large republics (France, Portugal, Switzerland)	Mean of 8.3 orders
Small republics (Andorra, San Marino)	0.5 orders

The republics evidently should be handled parallel with the monarchies, not as a low class at the bottom. The age of the state can also be expected to influence the number of orders, for reasons we have already discussed. We test this hypothesis in the following table, during the periods we previously introduced:

States or dynasties established before 1792 (38 states)	Mean of 5.2 orders
States established between 1811 and 1819 (4 states)	4.0 orders
States established between 1819 and 1832 (2 states)	4.5 orders
States established between 1832 and 1872 (2 states)	4.0 orders
States established between 1872 and 1914 (2 states)	4.0 orders

The differences are unexpected small. New states evidently considered orders as an important aspect of their sovereignty. But we still expect that states established after 1810 should have a lower proportion of the more old fashioned types of orders, such as high orders, military orders, orders for ladies, etc. We may divide the orders in nine different types and get the following table:

Mean number of orders (9 different kinds) in states established before 1792 and states established between 1810 and 1914 in Europe.

	States established in 1792	States established 1810—1914
1. High orders. Mean number per state	0,8	0.5
2. Orders of military merit	0.9	0.5
3. Orders for ladies	0.4	0.1
4. Orders of St. John, religion orders	0.3	0.2
5. Orders for art and science	0.2	0.1
6. Colonial orders	0.5	0.3
7. Orders for agriculture and industry	0.1	0
8. Orders open for civilians	1.4	2.0
9. Other kinds of orders (Red Cross, etc.)	0.6	0
Total of orders, mean number	5.2	4.1

The new states had more orders open to civilians than the old states, but of every other kind of orders they had less, expecially of orders for ladies, for art and science, for military merit and also less of the high orders.

This picture, however, is too simple. The political change in Europe had united Germany as well as Italy, while breaking up Turkey. This meant that many of the small states had been included in the German empire and that the new states were comparatively large. Small states thus tend to be old and this of course lowers the mean number of orders in the old states. If we want to compare old and new states, we should divide the old ones in states with full sovereignity and states without diplomatic representation, etc. We then get three classes of states: old, sovereign states, new sovereign states and old, not quite sovereign states. How do their orders differ?

Mean number of orders (9 kinds) in old and new sovereign states and old, non-sovereign states of 1914, before World War I.

	Sovereign states established		Not sovereign states
	before 1792	after 1810	
1. High orders. Mean number per state	2.2	0.5	0.2
2. Orders of military merit	1.3	0.5	0.3
3. Orders for ladies	0.8	0.1	0.3
4. Orders of St. John, religious orders	0.7	0.2	0
5. Orders for art and science	0.4	0.1	0.2
6. Colonial orders	1.8	0.2	0
7. Orders for agriculture and industry	0.4	0	0
8. Orders open to civilians	2.1	2.1	1.2
9. Other kinds of orders (Red Cross, etc.)	0.8	0.3	0.4
Total of orders, mean number	10.3	4.0	2.5
Number of states	12	10	26

This table demonstrates that the new states have surpassed the old states without full sovereignty, expecially in the number of orders open to civilians, but the new states still were far below the old sovereign states.

The European states thus have on one hand a strong tendency to build a large set of useful orders, but there is at the same time a strong tendency to curb excess, especially in small states. And then we want to know the actual distribution of the number of orders. The means are not enough.

We know that the number of orders in a state is associated with its rank, power, colonies, age and religion. We combine four of these traits, so that we start with the combination most favorable for orders and then step by step go down to the least favorable one. Some combinations are, however, not represented by states, and so we get only 16 combinations in table 1.

Table 1. Number of orders in European states of 1914, according to their rank, religion, age and sovereignty.

Combination of traits	states number	0	1	2	3—5	6—10	11—15	16—20	20	Mean
1. Empires, catholic, before 1810	1							1		17
2. Empires, non-catholic, before 1810	4					2	1	1		11.8
3. Kingdoms, catholic, before 1810, sovereign	2					1			1	14
4. Kingdoms, catholic, before 1810, nonsovereign	2					1	1			11
5. Kingdoms, catholic, after 1810, sovereign	1					1				7
6. Kingdoms, non-catholic, before 1810, sovereign	3			1	1	1				4.3
7. Kingdoms, non-catholic, before 1810, non-sovereign	2				1	1				5
8. Kingdoms, non-catholic, after 1810, sovereign	6			3	1	2				4.0
9. Grand duchy, catholic	1				1					3
10. Grand duchies, non-catholic, nonsovereign	6		2	2	2					2.3
11. Duchies, etc., catholic, non-sovereign	2	1	1							0.5
12. Duchies, etc., non-catholic, before 1810, non-sovereign	12		7	4	1					1.5
13. Duchies, etc., non-catholic, after 1810, sovereign	1		1							1
14. Republics, catholic, before 1810, sovereign	2				1			1		12
15. Republics, catholic, before 1810, non-sovereign	2	1	1							0.5
16. Republic, non-catholic, before 1810, sovereign	1	1								0

Table 2. Number of orders in European states of 1914, according to their rank, religion, age and sovereignty.

	No. of states	0	1	2	3—4	5—6	7—8	9—10	11—12	13—14	Mean
1. Empires, catholic, before 1810	1									1	13
2. Empires, non-catholic, before 1810	4						1	2	1		9.5
3. Kingdoms, catholic, before 1810, sovereign	2						1	1			9.0
4. Kingdoms, catholic, before 1810, non-sovereign	2						1	1			8.5
5. Kingdoms, catholic, after 1810, sovereign	1					1					5
6. Kingdoms, non-catholic, before 1810, sovereign	3			1		2					4.3
7. Kingdoms, non-catholic, before 1810, non-sovereign	2				2						3.5
8. Kingdoms, non-catholic, after 1810, sovereign	6		1	2	1	2					3.2
9. Grand duchy, catholic	1				1						3
10. Grand duchies, non-catholic, non-sovereign	6		2	2	2						2.7
11. Duchies, etc., catholic, non-sovereign	2	1	1								0.5
12. Duchies, etc., non-catholic, before 1810, non-sovereign	12		7	5							1.5
13. Duchies, etc., non-catholic, after 1810, sovereign	1		1								1
14. Republics, catholic, before 1810, sovereign	2				2						4
15. Republics, catholic, before 1810, non-sovereign	2	1	1								0.5
16. Republics, non-catholic, before 1810, sovereign	1	1									0

The table shows a definite pattern: the number of orders of a state depend in a predictable manner of its rank, religion, age and sovereignty. There are four cases falling out of the range: on line 3 Spain exceeds the expected number thanks to its unique set of medieval orders (probably without function in 1914) on line 6 where Denmark has established only two orders instead of the proper number 5—6, in line 11 where Liechtenstein had no orders instead of the one or two to be expected and eventually line 14, where France has an unreasonable number of colonial orders, not disturbing to the European market of orders but certainly upsetting our table.

We hold to our idea that the number of orders is an index of the adaptation of the state to its situation in Europe. We try then to omit the orders irrelevant to the situation of 1914 and simply exclude colonial orders and orders to be considered as historical relics, that is, orders for ladies and medieval orders, reserved for the old nobility (thus neither the Garter nor the Golden Fleece are excluded). The cleansed table is presented as table 2.

The states are grouped fairly close to the regression line, going from the upper, right corner to the lower, left corner, which means that we can predict the number of orders of any European country once we know the relevant data about its rank, religion, age and sovereignity, provided that we may exclude colonial orders, the orders reserved for ladies and the medieval orders reserved for the nobility of the country.

The orders and World War I

Our choice of 1914 makes it possible not only to study the system of European orders at that time but also to investigate the impact of World War I by looking at the new orders created during and because of the war. We then use our previous set of variables characterizing the states and relate them to orders, high orders, military orders, orders for ladies, but also for new orders, adapted to the stress of the war. We collect all these data in one, single table next page.

Rank of sovereign, political power, diplomatic rank, population, urbanization, colonies and participation in World War I all were associated with a system of orders and also with the creation of new orders during the war. Actually, no neutral state created any orders these years. It looks as if the variables density of population,

Table 3. Percentages of states possessing orders of different kinds and creating new orders during World War I.

States having:	No. of states June, 1914	% with orders June, 1914	% with high orders June, 1914	% with civil orders June, 1914	% with military orders June, 1914	% with ladies orders June, 1914	% with new ord. created in WW I
High rank sovereign	20	100	65	95	65	55	45
Lower rank	28	89	14	93	21	4	7
Political power	21	95	67	95	57	38	33
Little or no power	27	93	11	93	41	15	15
Diplomatic representation	20	95	65	95	60	40	35
No representation	28	93	14	93	25	14	14
Above 1 million	24	96	67	95	67	45	38
Below 1 million	24	92	4	92	13	4	8
Dense population	26	96	31	92	35	23	27
Less dense population	22	91	41	96	45	27	18
Urbanized states	21	100	33	95	48	24	33
Less urbanized	27	89	37	93	67	26	15
University	28	96	47	96	61	36	28
No university	20	90	20	90	10	10	15
Catholic religion	13	85	46	85	54	31	23
Non-catholic	35	97	32	97	34	23	32
Colonies	9	100	56	89	89	44	33
No colonies	39	92	31	95	28	21	21
Belligerent	36	100	31	100	42	31	31
Neutral	12	75	50	75	33	8	0
Sum	48	94	35	94	40	25	22

The European Orders before and during World War 1

university system and religion meant less than the other variables at this time.

There is little to glean from the columns about orders of all kinds and about civil orders, as all but three countries have got them. The high orders with a single class, however, are more associated with high ranking sovereigns, political power, diplomatic representation and size of population than with colonies, universities or religion. Still, states with more urbanization, population density and taking part in World War I actually have a *lower* percentage possessing high orders than the less urbanized, less densely populated and neutral states. The military orders show a similar pattern as the civilian orders, only in general with more clearcut differences.

The new orders, created during the war, were—as we have pointed out—created exclusively by the states taking part in the struggle, but among them high ranking sovereigns and populous states showed a stronger tendency to use orders as rewards.

Chapter 10
The Period between World War I and World War II

The five European empires had the highest rank and the best equipped sets of orders to compensate for their various weaknesses, still, during the first World War, these benefits could not compensate their deficits in blood and iron. Four of the five disappeared with the peace, leaving only the British empire still standing. Instead a set of new national states entered the European scene: Czeckoslovakia, Esthonia, Finland, Lithuania, Latvia and Poland, which had fought hard for their freedom, first with weapons and then at the peace conferences. The small German states were united in the new republic of Germany. Serbia and Montenegro together with parts of Austria-Hungary formed the kingdom of Yugoslavia. We distinguish between four different types of European states:

1. New national states and to them belongs Ireland after 1922.
2. Defeated states: Austria, Bulgaria (?), Germany, Hungary, Russia and Turkey.
3. Victorious states: Albania(?), Belgium, France, Great Britain, Greece, Italy, Luxemburg, Portugal, Rumania and Yugoslavia.
4. Neutral states: Andorra, Denmark, the Holy See, Liechtenstein, Monaco, Netherlands, Norway, San Marino, Spain, Sweden, and Switzerland.

We expect the new national states to create at the double pace one or two military orders each to reward the heroes of their struggle for liberty—and then some years later, to create orders for the civilians in civil service and diplomacy. The defeated states got rid of their dynasties with orders and all, which should bring about new orders. Bulgaria is a dubious case here, as they quickly changed sides towards the end of the war and thus escaped complete defeat, change of dynasty and could keep their orders. Still, we do not find it appropriate to label Bulgaria victorious. Albania is a doubtful victor, since it declared itself neutral.

The dynasties of the victorious states of course felt rather secure, had all their orders left and if they had need of new military orders they created them during the war, not after. But orders for civilians even the victorious states might need to reward merits in the work of reconstruction. The neutral states eventually should have little need of orders. They had neither taken part in the struggle nor changed their dynasties. We try this model in the following table:

Proportion of states in different categories creating orders for military merit and for civil merit in 1919—20 and in 1921—29.

Category of states	Proportion of states creating military orders		Proportion of states creating ord. for civilians	
	1919—20	1921—29	1919—20	1921—29
New national states	5/6	0/7	2/6	4/7
Defeated states	0/6	0/6	0/6	3/6
Victorious states	0/9	0/9	0/9	4/9
Neutral states	0/11	0/11	1/11	2/11

The only states creating military orders were the new national states in 1919—20. The victorious states already had rewarded their war heroes and the defeated states had little interest in rewarding beaten heroes. The neutral states were lucky enough to lack heroes. But the orders open also to civilians show another picture. Two of the new national states created civil orders already in 1919—20 and the remaining four in 1921—29. Ireland, however, dit not, and still has not created a real order. Three of the defeated states, Austria, Hungary and Soviet, instituted new orders open to civilians in 1921 —29 and so did four of the victorious states too. The neutral states should have less reasons to create any orders, and actually only one was created in 1919—20, two in 1921—29.

Singer and Small have given the diplomatic rank order of the states in 1925. We expect, of course, that the higher their rank, the more orders they should possess. See top table next page.

The highest rank group has the highest mean, the next group has the next highest mean, but then there are no differences until the lowest ranking group comes out with the lowest mean. But four middle groups with 16 states have the same mean, 2.5—2.8. These states evidently have standardized their set of orders.

"The economic consequences" of peace, splitting up the old economic interaction units of Austria and Russia in smaller, indepen-

Rank	Countries	Mean number of orders
1—4	Great Britain, France, Italy, Belgium	12.8
5—8	Germany, Spain, Netherlands, Norway	6.3
9—12	Switzerland, Austria, Denmark, Sweden	2.5
13—16	Poland, Portugal, Hungary, Turkey	2.8
17—20	Czechoslovakia, Rumania, Finland, Yugoslavia	2.5
21—24	Esthonia, Greece, Bulgaria, Livonia	2.8
25—29	Luxemburg, Soviet, Lithuania, Albania, Ireland	1.6

dent states, did not ease the European economy after World War I. The great depression hit Europe in 1930. The economic stress was severe and in many countries the political disturbances resulted in dictatorships establishing more or less authoritarian patterns, but also in rising taxes and lower pay to civil servants, etc. Here the orders were useful. They represent a cheap way to show appreciation and give status to those who could not be paid adequately in cash, and still were important to control, as these administrators in their turn were to control the citizens, these citizens increasingly difficult to handle. The new orders thus were meant to reward obediance rather than sense of duty, strictness rather than intelligence.

We try to test this point by dividing the European states in three classes: dictatorships, new national states (here including also Austria, Germany, Hungary, Soviet and Turkey) and the remaining states. But what to do with states belonging to more than one class? Italy, for instance, belonged to the class "remaining states" in 1921, but then was made a dictatorship, Germany in the same way was a new national state until Hitler took over in 1931, etc. We evidently have to reclassify the states each year and compute the number of new orders per state and year, if we are to make our comparison meaningful:

Creation of new orders per state and year in three classes of European states in 1921—1939.

Class of state	New orders per state and year
Dictatorships	.14
New national states	.06
Remaining states	.02

The dictatorships used the orders most efficiently or were forced to do so. The new national states still used orders far more than the remaning states, which after all already possessed well equipped sets of orders and probably also were better off economically.

The European Orders in 1922

The new orders, created between the two world wars, we have tried to cover, but we still have to show what the European sets of orders looked like in, say 1922, since several states, important from our point of view (orders), are gone and the new states followed different patterns.

We choose the year 1922 as the year showing the new Europe, but when it comes to the orders we take care of those created between 1922 and 1939 and place them in a special column. Singer and Small do not give the diplomatic rank of the states until in 1925, but this is no serious draw back. And in 1922 it is no longer any use to differentiate between orders of the old kinds. We just register which countries have or have not orders, created or did not create new orders. See table 1, next page.

The table demonstrates what we might have expected. The monarchies possessed orders to a higher proportion than the republics, many of which were created in the peace of Versailles and not yet accustomed to the peculiar sets of rules regulating interaction between and within states. But the republics in the following years created more orders than the monarchies, to make up for their deficit.

The dictatorial states generally already had from the beginning a higher proportion of states possessing orders, but they still created new orders in a far higher proportion than did the democratic states.

The states with a higher diplomatic rank in 1925—according to Singer and Small—not only had a higher proportion of states possessing orders, but also a higher proportion of states creating new orders, which is a bit of a surprise.

The old, established states had, of course, a far higher proportion of states with orders, but the new states then showed a far higher proportion of states creating new orders in 1922—1939.

Size of population is an important factor and this time so many of the small states have been included in larger countries, that we have to draw the line between larger and smaller states at the six

Table 1. Percentages of states possessing orders in 1922 and creating new orders in 1922—1939.

States having:	No. of states	% with orders	% creating new orders
Monarchical government	16	88 %	50 %
Republican government	18	55 %	77 %
Dictatorships established 1921—39	16	81 %	88 %
Dictatorships not established	18	61 %	44 %
Higher diplomatic rank	17	83 %	71 %
Lower diplomatic rank	17	59 %	59 %
States established before World War I	20	85 %	50 %
States established after World War I	14	50 %	86 %
Population above 6 million	18	83 %	77 %
Population below 6 million	16	58 %	50 %
More urbanized states	15	80 %	53 %
Less urbanized states	19	63 %	74 %
Dense population	17	83 %	65 %
Less dense population	17	59 %	65 %
With universities	27	74 %	71 %
Without universities	7	57 %	43 %
Colonies	7	100 %	71 %
No colonies	27	63 %	63 %
Sum	34	71 %	65 %

million mark. The eighteen more populous states have, of course, a higher proportion of states with orders already in 1922, but in spite of this they also had a higher proportion states creating orders in the following years.

We have drawn the line for urbanization so that fifteen states are to be considered as more urbanized, nineteen as less urbanized. The more urbanized states also had a higher proportion of states with orders and a lower proportion of states creating new orders in the times up to World War II.

States with higher population density we defined as those above 65 inhabitants per square kilometer, in order to get seventeen states above this mark and seventeen below. The states with higher density had a higher proportion of states possessing orders in 1922, but when we turn to the creation of new orders, there is no difference between the more dense and the less dense states.

Universities in 1922 belonged to the set of necessities only very small states were unable to afford, and there were no more than seven of them: Albania, Andorra, the Holy See, Liechtenstein, Luxemburg, Monaco and San Marino. These small states not only lacked universities but also tended to lack orders and to show little interest in creating new ones.

Seven states at this time still possessed colonies: Belgium, France, Great Britain, Italy, Netherlands, Portugal and Spain. All of them also had orders and five of them also created new orders before World War II.

We would generally expect that states possessing orders would have less need of new orders. This, however, does not hold for the dictatorships, the states with high diplomatic rank, large populations, universities or colonies. But in order to analyse these interacting factors, we have to use a more complicated and rather tedious technique, which we postpone to our last chapter.

Orders during World War II

We expect World War II to repeat the pattern from World War I closely: the belligerent nations using new orders to exhibit and reward heroship and loyalty, the neutral states creating no new orders, as there were no reasons to make extra orders for the little extra amount of heroship or loyalty needed. These war rewards should have more use for military than for civil orders and be

Proportion of states creating military orders and civilian orders during World War II, states according to power and activity in the war.

Type of States	Proportion of states creating in World War II	
	Military orders	Civil orders
Great powers	5/5	3/5
Other belligerent states	4/17	3/17
Neutral states	1/9	1/9
Sum	10/31	7/31

more used by great powers than by belligerent nations of less prominence.

To test this, we should, however, reduce our number of states from 34 to 31, as Albania, Czechoslovakia and Austria were occupied already before the beginning of the war. The data then can be given in the last table of this chapter.

The military orders were used by all great powers, a quarter of the other nations taking part in the war and one single neutral nation, Spain. The civil orders were, as we found already in data from World War I, used less, but still by three out of five great powers, three out of seventeen other belligerent nations and Spain alone among the nine neutral nations.

Chapter 11
The European States after World War II and Their Orders

A European country's constitution in 1945 depended entirely upon which power had last occupied the country. The same was true for the orders. The Russian-occupied countries should follow the Soviet Union's order-happy pattern in conferment of military as well as civil merit orders. The states occupied by the allies had no reasons to institute new military orders, as those merits were no merits at all from the allies' point of view, but all the more reason for instituting civil orders for those who served the new state and its new administration. The German-occupied at the end of the occupation just returned to their former patterns and had moderate reasons to complement their old orders with new—unless they especially wanted to reward prominent members of the Underground. The fighting, non-occupied states had had ample chances to institute the new orders they needed during the war and should rarely do so afterwards. Finally, the neutral states should also show sparing. We test this in the table:

Proportion of states of different types which instituted military merit orders, resp. civil merit orders, during the period 1945—54.

Type of occupation	Proportion of states which 1945—54 instituted	
	military merit orders	civil merit orders
Last occupied by Russians	5/8	7/8
Last occupied by Allies	0/4	3/4
Last occupied by Germans	2/7	2/7
Belligerent, not occupied	0/5	0/5
Neutral	1/9	1/9

During this period Spain instituted new orders (intended for Africa), which breaks the neutral states' nil. The pattern otherwise supports our expectations well.

The Conferment of Orders during the Period 1955—64

Here we choose to place the five colonial powers in a separate group with strong needs for orders. The strongly-controlled easternblock countries, Bulgaria, Rumania, Czechoslovakia, Hungary and East Germany, place civil servants likewise as the buffer between government and citizens, which job should be compensated with orders. The less strongly bound east-block countries are in a better position, and should therefore institute less orders. The remaining states should show restraint in the creation of new orders. We can test these hypotheses in the following table:

The proportion of states of different types which instituted new military merit resp. civil merit orders, during the period 1955—64.

Type of states	Proportion of states which 1955—64 instituted	
	military merit orders	civil merit orders
Colonial powers	2/5	3/5
Strongly-bound eastern states	2/5	3/5
Less strongly-bound eastern states	0/4	2/4
Other states	0/19	4/19

Our hypotheses are supported. But it is interesting that all types of states seem to create more civil merit orders than military merit orders—even the colonial powers.

Lipset has suggested that states be divided into stable and unstable (Political Man, Anchor Books, P. 32), giving for the European states, 14 stable and 22 unstable. We expect, of course, that the stable will be more sparing with new orders than the unstable, which are trying to achieve stability also through the application of new orders. See table next page.

Lipset's division proves to be relevant in this connection too. It would however, be interesting to illustrate the interaction between

Proportion of stable and unstable states (acc. to Lipset) which instituted new military resp. civil merit orders, during the ten-year period 1955—64.

Type of states	Proportion of states which 1955—64 instituted	
	military merit orders	civil merit orders
Stable states	0/14	3/14
Unstable states	4/20	10/20

the different variables in more detail. And so let us try another technique than the tables we have used previously. Instead of presenting percentages, we try to show the strength of association between the states' possession of orders and other variables characterizing the states. Which variables can we use this way?

We have access to eleven such variables, but unfortunately we lack diplomatic representation. Singer and Small have computed it up to 1940, but not later. The remaining eleven variables for the 33 states will be:

1. *The state's age.* The sixteen states which existed in 1914 and had not changed their type of government since then were considered older, the remaining seventeen as younger.
2. *The state's rank.* The twelve monarchies were given higher rank than the twenty-one republics.
3. *The state's stability.* Those states which Lipset considered unstable were included as such, and the remaining as stable.
4. *Urbanization.* Seventeen states we considered more urbanized and sixteen less urbanized.
5. *Density of population.* Was higher in seventeen states and lower in sixteen.
6. *Population.* We based this on the population figures for 1950/51, and drew the line at 7.2 million in order to obtain seventeen states with large populations and sixteen states with small populations.
7. *Universities* were established in 26 states, lacking in seven small states.
8. *Colonies* now belonged only to six states, since Italy had lost hers.
9. *War participation and neutral states.* Twenty-four states had

taken part in World War II and only nine could be considered neutral.

10. *Occupying power.* We divide the states in those occupied by Russians and/or allied powers and on the other hand in those occupied by Germans or not occupied.

11. *Dictatorships.* We consider that Turkey, Greece, Spain, Portugal and the eastern-block countries are dictatorships and the remaining twenty not.

We give the correlation coefficients between these variables on one hand and on the other their possession of orders in 1945 and their creation of new orders since 1945 (coefficients computed as Yule's coefficients):

Table 1.

Variable	Correlation with	
	possession of orders 1945	creation of new orders later
1. The state's age	+.89	—.68
2. The state's rank	+1	—.53
3. The state's stability	+.67	—.51
4. Urbanization	+.57	—.06
5. Density of population	+.57	—.06
6. Size of population	—.42	+.68
7. Possession of university	—.29	+.55
8. Possession of colonies	+1	—.04
9. War participation	—.26	+.71
10. Occupying power	—.91	+.93
11. Dictatorships	—.58	+.95

Possession of orders in 1945 thus was more common in high ranking, colonial, old, stable, urbanized and densely populated European states, while the states occupied by Russians and/or allied forces, or here classified as dictatorships, populous, with universities established, or taking part in the war, tended to lack orders. On the whole, states lacking orders in 1945, tried to compensate this the following years up till now, as all variables positively correlated with possession of orders in 1945 were negatively correlated with the creation of new orders afterwards and vice versa.

Looking at the table, it is easy to say that colonies and rank seem to be very important factors for the orders as possession of orders and creation of new ones both were correlated with these variables. But a statistician would immediately look for the correlation between rank and colonies. If all the colonial states had high rank, there would be just one factor, not two. Are we to analyze the interaction between our eleven variables above, on one hand, possession of orders and creation of new orders on the other, we actually should look into the interaction between *all* the variables.

This can be done by computing all the correlations between our total number of 11 state variables and 2 order variables, these 13 variables having 78 intercorrelation with one another, which we present in the following table or correlation matrix. Table 2.

The matrix shows that the first five variables, age, rank, stability, possession of orders and of colonies form a cluster, that is, are very closely associated with one another; that the last five variables: size of population, war participation, occupation by Russian and/or allied forces, dictatorial governments and creation of new orders also were closely associated with one another, but forming a second cluster of their own, as they were *not* associated with the first five; on the contrary: twenty-three of the twenty-five correlations between the five variables in the first cluster and the five in the second are negative. Then eventually, we have three variables in the middle: possession of universities, urbanization and density of population associated with both clusters and so intermediate between them.

Technically we can handle this situation easily by changing the last five variables, turning them up side down (changing their direction), by redefining them as small, handy populations instead of large, neutral instead of belligerent in World War II, occupied by Germans or not occupied instead of occupied by Russians and/or allied forces, as democratic instead of dictatorial, needing no new orders instead of creating them. Then, of course, the first five and the last five would immediately form one big happy cluster with just two negative correlations out of fifty-five.

We do not, however, accept that solution, as some of these variables look silly turned upside down; for instance population size looks more reasonable in the direction from small populations to large ones, creation of new orders indicates an interesting activity, while no new orders indicate absence of this activity, etc. And if we retain the two original clusters, not changing the directions in one of them, we are able to use the summation theory to study the interaction

Table 2. Matrix of the correlations (Yule's coefficients) between 13 variables, characterizing 33 European States after World War II.

Variables	1. Age	2. Rank	3. Stability	4. Possession of orders	5. Colonies
1. Age of state		+.94	+.82	+.89	+.76
2. Rank of state			+.91	+.1	+.65
3. Stability (Lipset)				+.67	+.55
4. Possessin of orders					+1
5. Colonies					
6. Universities					
7. Urbanization					
8. Density of population					
9. Size of population					
10. War participation					
11. Occupying power					
12. Dictatorships					
13. Creation of new orders					
weight	+.42	+.32	+.22	+.24	—.13

more closely. This "theory" was introduced by Boalt in *Family and Marriage* (McKay, New York 1965) to discuss the selection in marriage and then in *Sociology of Research* (Southern Illinois University Press, Carbondale, 1969) to analyze the interaction of scientific values. The general idea goes something like this: the researcher is anxious to make his project correspond as far as possible to a number of scientific values, such as a strong theoretical basis, scientific literature in the field well covered, an efficient statistical technique and use to society. We would then expect that the researcher strengthening his theoretical basis would also have to dig deeper in the literature and so would cover both of these values with the same behavior, but this would not give him a statistical technique, which he would have to grasp with quite other means. And his research results could hardly be of real use to society unless they could be generalized according to statistical rules. Probably his exertions to secure a good statistical technique would also help him to make his results useful to society but hardly to strengthen his theory or cover the literature in the special field more efficiently. And, as researchers have limited resources of money, time and energy, they would have to decide how to allocate their resources between the two competing

6. Universities	7. Urbanization	8. Density of population	9. Size of population	10. War participation	11. Occupying power	12. Dictatorships	13. Creation of new orders
+.81	+.60	+.41	—.68	—.71	— 1	—.86	—.68
+.43	+.35	+.77	—.53	—.71	— 1	—.69	—.53
+.45	+.83	+.41	—.51	—.06	—.74	— 1	—.51
—.29	+.57	+.57	—.42	—.26	—.91	—.58	—.62
+1	+.37	+.37	+ 1	+.36	— 1	—.16	—.04
	—.14	—.14	+ 1	+.43	+.58	+.88	+.55
		+,96	+.06	+.47	+.09	—.80	+.06
			+.29	+.47	+.35	—.71	+.06
				+.88	+.66	+.86	+.68
					+ 1	+.78	+.71
						+.73	+.93
							+.95
—.45	—.43	—.40	+.02	+.16	+.68	+.40	+.32

clusters of scientific values we presented as as illustration. Now let us try to apply this general technique to our own problem.

The Summation Theory Applied to Our Problem

We then consider the states as organizations trying to achieve a number of goals or values. We have little opportunity to cover or to indicate their different kinds of goals or values. Actually, we have just selected them out of a small number, because they looked promising and were not too difficult to estimate with our simple tools and so we have introduced them as our thirteen variables. But can we really label these variables as values of the state-organization? Let us try.

The age of the organization certainly can be seen as a value, associated with traditions, accepted forms for handling conflicts and stresses, certain reserves built into the organization and the chance to socialize the members along these lines.

The rank of the sovereign is, of course, a value as monarchs after all have a halo around their crowns, anointed with holy oil, carrying the symbols of crown, orb, spire and sword, being the centers of ceremonies and mass media. The higher rank, the more status also to the state or organization.

Stability in Lipset's sense, of course, is a value to any organization.

Possession of orders means that the organization has an accepted and appreciated technique to give status to persons not only in need of it but also in their rights, from the organization's point of view, to receive this kind of status. This means that the leaders of the organization get more rewards to distribute and they acquire this addition of rewards at a comparatively low cost. The total sum of rewards is thus increased, which undoubtedly should be valuable to the organization.

Colonies have once been valuable and, of course, the colonial states would not have invested in colonies or still retain colonies, unless they considered them valuable. But we admit that there is an inflation in colonies now.

Universities are rather necessary service branches to the state organizations, providing them with specialists of different kinds.

Urbanization can be seen as a value of a state, as the concentration of people is bound up with industrialization and concentration of contacts, raising production and communication, that is, contributing to bringing down the price of things and contacts.

Density of population is a value very near to urbanization.

Size of population is a convenient measure of the organization itself, but then the organizations with many members also tend to get more resources, more specialists, and generally more power.

War participation is a doubtful value here. Most of the states going into World War II preferred war to other possible lines of actions and so war for them can be considered a value. But some states were occupied, quickly or slowly, without getting a chance to choose. What was the value of the war to them? Well, if we change the direction and say that neutrality is the value, we are no better off, as the neutral states did not have much of a choice either, possibly to declare war on Germany in the last days of the war. And so we prefer to consider that those fighting the enemy did so because they gave a higher value to fighting than to submitting.

Occupying power certainly left very little to the free choice of the occupied country. But once occupied, they all adapted, in one way during the war, in another and more definite way after the war. Such an adaptation brings about a series of changes meant to ease and rationalize the occupation as a political system and political leaders sympathetical to the occupants, a redefinition of history and traditions according to the new siutation. In the long run, the occupants probably run the risk to be classified as negative values, but in the short run the government, and the new topmen owe their promotion and status to the occupants thus—for some time— hailing them as values.

Dictatorships in the same way are valuable as they have replaced chaos or democracy—from their point of view identical—and then had opportunity to change the forms of the government, to select its members, to have history rewritten and education redefined as it best suited the needs of the dictator.

Creation of new orders, of course, is a value to the state-organization if it brings a considerable addition of respected rewards to be distributed by the head of the state.

We have thus tried to demonstrate that our thirteen variables can be considered values. The matrix of the intercorrelations between these thirteen values shows, that they form two different clusters, the first five forming one cluster, the last five another.

This might mean that our state-organizations, allocating their resources in many different ways, have crystallized a cluster of reactions, characterized by the set of values to be attained: age, rank and stability of state, possession of colonies—and of orders (and maybe universities). On the other hand states, unable or unwilling to react this way, tend to be served another set reactions and values: large populations, participation in war, occupation by Russian or allies, dictatorships and creation of new orders, the last value actually the only value in the second cluster really efficient, as creation of new orders certainly is able to compensate lack of old orders. To this second cluster, we also, with some hesitation, add the values of urbanization and density of population as these two variables after all seem to have a little more in common with the second cluster, especially the value of population size.

This neat little sketch probably will not convince many historians. And they are right. The truth can hardly be as simple as this. Too many of the really important variables or values have been excluded. Yes, quite, but please remember that we are not trying to rewrite European history, we are only trying to demonstrate what happened to the European orders of knighthood. We have chosen a small number of variables, hoping they will shred some light on the creation of orders.

Well, then our information about the orders seems to be concentrated in the two opposing clusters of values, the first cluster containing the traditional values and the existing orders, the second cluster containing values of change, including creation of new orders. And from the summation theory we take over the viewpoint, that all reactions of the states might be considered as adaptations, and in part as adaptations to one another. If the country lacks political stability, changing cabinets quickly, dictatorship might be considered a substitute for stability, or the strong neighbor might try an occupation, etc. But in order to convince the historians that this viewpoint can be used, we would need for more and far more relevant values.

We are, however, anxious to demonstrate the technique of the summation theory, even though our set of values is far from the ideal. So let us go on and try to find some measure of the strength of the values we have tried to handle. The summation theory tackles the problem of measuring the total strength of values this way: if for instance stability is an important value, then lack of it would mean that many states would have to replace it or compensate it with reactions, and the more and the stronger these reactions are, the more important stability would appear to be. These compensatory reactions would, however, appear mainly or exclusively in the second cluster and so we suggest that we measure the strength of our values by computing their mean correlation with the values *excluded* from their own cluster. Thus the importance or *weight* of stability would be the mean of $+.83$, $+.41$, $-.51$, $-.06$, $-.74$, -1 and $-.51$. This mean is $-.22$, but as the negative sign here actually means that stability is negatively correlated with the values of the second cluster, that is, has to be compensated by them, high weights computed this way will always be negative, which seems impractical. For this reason, we always change the sign of the mean. High weights thus always are made positive this way. The weight of stability then is $+22$.

This does not mean that all weights turn out with positive signs. Take for instance the value of universities, with some hesitation included in the first of our two clusters as it has strong positive correlations with four of the five other variables in this cluster. But at the same time it has positive correlations also with five of the seven variables in the second cluster. The mean of the seven correlations between universities and the second cluster then is positive, $+.45$, and changing the sign, as it should be changed, the university variable is given the weight of —.45. Low weight, showing that the variable has little or no effect in the interaction with variables outside its own cluster, thus will not be zero, but negative, if computed this way.

We must realize, however, that these weights are easily changed by introducing new variables or excluding some of those we already have. If we, for instance, exclude the three variables 6. universities, 7. urbanization and 8. density of population, we would eliminate 15 out of the 17 positive correlations between the variables of the first cluster with the variables of the second, which would raise the weights of the remaining ten variables considerably. Then prudence makes it necessary not to pay to much attention to the numerical value of the weights. Probably it is more important which cluster they belong to and which rank they possess in the order of their cluster. Thus, the variables of the first cluster should be ranked: 1. Age, 2. Rank, 3. Possession of orders, 4. Stability, 5. Colonies, and 6. Universities. The second cluster's variables then evidently are: 1. Occupation power, 2. Dictatorship, 3. New orders, 4. Participation in World War II, 5. Size of population, 6. Density of population, and 7. Urbanization.

Looking at these lists we have to realize that they demonstrate the weight of our variables in their interaction with one another in the matrix, not their weights according to other rules. Take for instance urbanization. Historians and sociologists probably would agree that this is an exceedingly important factor in the historical change of Europe. But it seems to be just as important to both of our two competing reaction patterns—and so it does not influence them and should have low weight. Weight here thus means just weight in the part of the interaction we are studying—not weight from other points of view.

But how are then our weights in interaction related to weight in other sense? That is difficult to say. We find it after all nearly impossible to rank factors according to their importance unless we have a very clear idea of what they should be important to. It is much easier to say that during the change this or that factor loses in importance while this one gains. And so we might try to study how the weights of our variables have changed, from 1792 to 1810, etc. We now wish that we had used the same set of variables all the time. But Lipset has not listed the stable nations until after World War II and so his variable is useless before that time. Loyalty to

Napoleon was a very important value in 1810 and may have retained some importance in 1819, but after that time it no longer is of interest, etc. We evidently have to admit, that the relevant variables may be substituted from time to time. And so, let us see what we can do with our data from 1792, 1810, 1819, 1832, 1872, 1914 and 1925.

Matrix Construction and Weight Computation for Our Previous Studies

We do not trust the patience of our readers to give attention to the details in seven more correlation matrices, and so we place them according to year in the remaining pages. We have already given the definitions of the variables we have used, the description of the statistical technique and the way to compute the interaction weights. All we have to do is to demonstrate the end results of our research in a table, giving the weights of the variables we have used to study the change of the European orders.

But some of the results are more difficult to cope with than we expected. In three matrices, those of 1792, 1832 and 1872, all the variables but one are united in the first cluster, thus leaving the single variable to the second cluster making our computions of the weights shaky as they, all but one, rest on one observation each. We would accept that, if the variable which alone makes up the second cluster, has a high proportion of strong negative correlations with the variables in the first cluster (which is the case in the matrix of 1832), but hardly otherwise. So when it comes to the point, we are unable to compute the weights in 1792 and 1872, but for the single variable in the second cluster. The weights we can get we present in table 3.

The most important point here is to point out the variables forming the second cluster, contrasting against or opposed to the first cluster, consisting of the traditional European political values: Diplomatic representation, Political power, Age of state, Stability, Colonies, Universities, Possession of orders and—for some time—Size of population. Then evidently the opposed second cluster in one sense can be considered a kind of threat to the traditional values of the strong European states. In 1792, only privileged nobility can be said to represent the last remnants of the feudal resistance to centralized

Variables	1792	1810	1819	1832	1872	1914	1925	1946
Loyalty to Metternich			+.42	+.59				
Loyalty to Napoleon		+.46	+.54					
Privileged nobility	—.15	+.53	—.30					
Dominant catholic religion		+.34	+.14	+1		+.23		
Diplomatic representation			+.33	+.6		+.44	+.06	
Political power		+.60	+.85	+.8		+.46		
Age of state							+7.4	+.42
Stability								+.22
Colonies		+.50	+1	+1		—.01	+.12	—.13
Universities		+.14	+.58	+.5		—.09	—.64	—.45
Orders of Knighthood		+.58	+.38	+.7		—.81	+.14	+.24
Creation of new orders						—.58	+.21	+.32
Dictatorships							+.18	+.68
Size of population		+.83	+.77	+.8		+.16	—.14	+.02
Urbanization				+.2	—.21	—.19	—.26	—.43
Density of population						+.18	+.39	—.40
Active participation war						—.02		+.16
Occupation power								+.68

Values within the closed areas belong to the second cluster. Opposed to the values of the first clusters: age of state, stability, etc.

monarchies, successfully preventing at least the German unification and the Italian one and thus associated with the small, powerless principalities, lacking diplomatic representation, colonies, universities, etc. In 1810, the value of loyalty to Napoleon is added to the second cluster, as the surviving German small states, most of them still sticking to their noble privileges, were united in the Confederation of the Rhine, a loyal tool to Napoleon. But in 1819, privileged

Table 4. Matrix of correlations (Yule's coefficients) between 8 variables characterizing 62 European states in 1792.

Variables	1. Rank of state	2. Political power	3. Size of population	4. Dominant religion	5. Colonies	6. Orders of knight-hood	7. Univer-sities	8. Privileged nobility
1. Rank of state, according to its head		+1	+1	+.19	+1	+.71	+.95	—.25
2. Political power of state			+1	+.26	+1	+.77	+.95	—.29
3. Size of population				+.33	+1	+.80	+.93	—.25
4. Dominant religion					+.14	+.42	—.27	—.30
5. Colonies						+.74	+1	+.79
6. Possession of orders of knighthood							+.66	+1
7. Universities								+.36
8. Privileged nobility								
Weight, as rank		2		1	6	7	5	

Table 5. Matrix of correlations (Yule's coefficients) between 9 variables characterizing 56 European states in 1810.

Variables	1. Rank of state	2. Political power	3. Size of population	4. Dominant religion	5. Colonies	6. Orders of knighthood	7. Universities	8. Privileged noiblity	9. Loyalty to Napoleon
1. Rank of state, according to its head		+.87	+.94	+.26	+1	+.99	+.84	−.70	−.21
2. Political power			+.92	+.09	+1	+.79	+.87	−.45	−.75
3. Size of population				+.18	+1	+.93	+.93	−.94	−.72
4. Dominant religion					+.24	+.29	−.06	−.30	−.38
5. Colonies						+1	+1	−.48	−.52
6. Orders of knighthood							+.32	−.67	−.49
7. Universities								−.13	−.15
8. Privileged nobility									+.35
9. Loyalty to Napoleon									
Weight of interaction	+.46	+.60	+.83	+.34	+.50	+.58	+.14	+.53	+.46

Table 6. Matrix of correlations (Yule's coefficients) between 11 variables characterizing 56 European states in 1819.

Variables	1. Rank of state	2. Political power	3. Diplomatic repre- sentation	4. Size of population
1. Rank of state		+.95	+.98	+.98
2. Political power			+.98	+.1
3. Diplomatic representation				+.99
4. Size of population				
5. Dominant religion				
6. Colonies				
7. Orders of knighthood				
8. Universities				
9. Privileged nobility				
10. Loyalty to Napoleon in 1810				
11. Loyalty to Metternich in 1819				
Weight of interaction	+.58	+.85	+.33	+.77

nobility drops out of the second cluster and instead is incorporated in the first. The dynasties once in 1810 loyal to Napoleon still form a useful variable influencing sets of orders, etc. but positively so strongly associated with loyalty to Metternich that these two variables together make up the second cluster—opposing the traditional set of European political values (an idea very alien to Metternich himself). In 1832, the Loyalty to Metternich is the one variable in the second cluster—still in opposition to traditional values, but in 1872, Metternich long ago is gone and then urbanization (and probably industrialization) makes up the second cluster alone. This is no coincidence, since in 1914 the second cluster of opposing variables also contains the urbanization variable with the variables Density of population and Participation in World War I added. Then Orders and New orders have so strong negative weights in the first cluster, that they must be near the second one.

This is theoretically interesting as the industrial factor and war here are coming as opposed to the traditional values and partly supported also by so traditional values as orders. But please remember, that now Europe was nearly completely covered with orders: the three little countries still without are not enough to ensure a reasonable amount of interaction between orders and the remaining

5. Dominant religion	6. Colonies	7. Orders of knighthood	8. Universities	9. Privileged nobility	10. Loyalty to Napoleon in 1810	11. Loyalty to Metternich in 1819
+.15	+1	+.93	+.95	+.54	—.60	—.55
+.27	+1	+.82	+.71	+.34	—.95	—.74
+.18	+1	+.91	+.71	+.37	—.03	—.62
+.33	+1	+.91	+.89	+.30	—.82	—.72
	+.32	+.21	—.30	+.21	—.28	±.0
		+ 1	+1	+.27	—1	—1
			+.83	+.80	—.53	—.23
				+.09	—.62	—.54
					—.03	+.62
						+1
+.14	+1	+.38	+.58	—.30	+.54	+.42

variables, and so the weight is negative.

In 1925, the small German principalities are gone, with orders and all. Instead, the new national states emerge. And the second cluster in about 1925 then is made up of rather large states, liable to be taken over by dictators—and often creating new orders. These three variables also form part of the second cluster in 1946, but to them are added Urbanization, Density of population, Participation in World War II and Occupation by Russian or allied troops. An alert reader might identify our two clusters in 1946, the first with the values still to some degree cherished in Western European countries, the second with those values more important to countries accepting values from behind the Iron Curtain. Observe, however, that industrialization, as measured by urbanization and density of population probably is given nearly as much regard in both sets of values.

Our discussion then indicated that most of the traditional political values in Europe tend to decrease in weight. Religion certainly decreases and we consider it unimportant after 1925, Diplomatic representation, Political power, Age of state, Colonies, Universities and Size of population, all of them tend to get lower weights, having less effect in the interaction with one another. But what about orders,

The European States after World War II and Their Orders   145

The European States after World War II and Their Orders

Table 7. Matrix of correlations (Yule's coefficient) between ten variables, characterizing 57 European states in 1832.

Variables	1. Rank of state	2. Political power	3. Diplomatic representation	4. Size of population	5. Dominant religion	6. Colonies	7. Urbanization	8. Orders of knighthood	9. Universities	10. Loyalty to Metternich
1. Rank of state		+.96	+.98	+.98	+.13	+1	+.29	+.97	+.95	−.58
2. Political power			+1	+1	+.32	+1	+.29	+.98	+.76	−.77
3. Diplomatic representation				+.99	+.24	+1	+.22	+.99	+.76	−.64
4. Size of population					+.24	+1	+.38	+.98	+.79	−.82
5. Dominant religion						+.19	+.29	+.28	−.18	−.06
6. Colonies							+.27	+1	+1	−1
7. Urbanization								+.77	+.44	−.24
8. Orders of knighthood									+.90	−.68
9. Universities										−.54
10. Loyalty to Metternich										
Weight, as rank	6	3	5	2	9	1	8	4	7	

Table 8. Matrix of correlations (Yule's coefficient) between 9 variables characterizing 45 European states in 1872.

Variables	1.' Rank of state	2. Political power	3. Diplomatic represen- tation	4. Orders of knight- hood	5. Colonies	6. Dominant religion	7. Univer- sities	8. Size of population	9. Urbaniza- tion
1. Rank of state		+.82	+.92	+1	+.71	+.17	+.85	+.85	−.10
2. Political power			+1	+.22	+1	+.37	+.60	+1	−.07
3. Diplomatic representation				+.99	+1	+.37	+.90	+1	−.07
4. Orders of knighthood					+1	−.46	+.22	+.01	+1
5. Colonies						+.35	+1	+1	+.84
6. Dominant religion							−.13	+.08	−.11
7. Universities								+.93	+.11
8. Size of population									+.05
9. Urbanization									
Weight									−.21

Variables	1. Rank of state	2. Political power	3. Diplomatic rank	4. Orders of knighthood	5. Colonies
1. Rank of state		+.94	+.90	+1	+7.5
2. Political power			+1	+.23	+1
3. Diplomatic rank				+.19	+1
4. Orders of knighthood					+1
5. Colonies					
6. Dominant religion					
7. Universities					
8. New orders created during war					
9. Size of population					
10. Density of population					
11. Urbanization					
12. Active part in World War I					
Weight	+.12	+.46	+.44	—.81	—.01

the center of our interest? Well, their weight decreases and is very small in 1914, but then they recover, new states use them or do not use them. Their weight is increasing, already in 1925 positive and still higher in 1946, when the countries behind the Iron Curtain started using orders on a large scale. This is reflected in the creation of new orders, in 1914 still belonging to the first cluster, of traditional values, but then included in the second cluster and gaining in weight.

And that is the end of our analysis. We have seen the use of orders increase in the traditional great powers with rank of empire and in the colonial powers. Both of them needed to compensate officers and civil servants for their labors and loyalty in a large bureaucracy. This pattern survived World War I, but when later on the state authority tightened its' grip of government, economy and organizations, it formed new patterns for loyalty among the civil servants, as well as new patterns for duties, rights and rewards, in order to

6. Dominant religion	7. Universities	8. New orders created during war	9. Size of population	10. Density of population	11. Urbanization	12. Active part in World War I
+.13	+.80	+.83	+.98	—.46	—.30	+.41
—.07	+.72	+.48	+.95	—.65	—.37	—.37
+.13	+.80	+.53	+.98	—.59	—.30	—.42
—.72	+.50	+1	+.35	+.43	+1	+1
+.66	+1	+.32	+1	+.03	+.52	—.51
	—.13	+.01	+.11	—.22	+.27	—.75
		+.39	+.94	—.03	+.30	±0
			+.74	+.27	+.48	+1
				—.33	+.08	—.22
					+.93	+.52
						+.28
+.23	—.09	—.58	+.16	+.18	—.19	—.02

single them out and to some degree compensate them for their stressed situation, squeezed between a harsh government and ungrateful subjects. Orders have traditionally been used this way and now they are created by states with this new official pattern. We then can use orders and the institution of new orders as a convenient indication of some factors in the political process.

We have applied the summation theory to make a closer study of this process and we have demonstrated how to use it. But, this is only a demonstration of a technique and the results are just examples. If we had just more variables, relevant for the problem, our results might have come out a great deal changed. So, we realize very well, that the European orders are of small importance, but consider them well adapted for a demonstration of macrosociological techniques, including the application of the summation theory and the study of time series.

Table 10. Matrix of correlations (Yule's coefficients) between 11 variables, characterizing 34 European states 1925—28.

Variables	1. Rank of state	2. Age of state	3. Diplomatic representation	4. Orders of knighthood
1. Rank of state		+.87	+.45	+.90
2. Age of state			±.0	+.77
3. Diplomatic representation				−.13
4. Orders of knighthood				
5. Colonies				
6. Urbanization				
7. Size of population				
8. Density of population				
9. Universities				
10. Dictatorship before 1939				
11. New orders created 1922—39				
Weight in interaction	+.60	+.74	+.06	+.14

5. Colonies	6. Urbaniz- ation	7. Size of pop- ulation	8. Density of population	9. Universi- ties	10. Dictator- ship before 1939	11. New orders created 1922—39
+.57	+.22	+.19	—.15	– .25	—.55	—.64
+1	+.67	+.10	+.24	—.70	—.71	—.76
+1	+,68	+.77	+.70	+1	±.0	—.12
+1	+.46	+.46	+.53	+.36	—.22	—.06
	+.73	+.1	+.1	+.73	—.11	—.12
		+.22	+.92	+.03	+.94	—.42
			+.23	+1	+.55	—.28
				—.18	—.77	±.0
					+.76	+.52
						+.94
+.12	—.26	—.14	+.33	—.64	+.18	+.21

Index of Orders